How to Write for Christian Magazines

How to Write
for
CHRISTIAN
MAGAZINES

Chip Ricks & Marilyn Marsh

BROADMAN PRESS
Nashville, Tennessee

© Copyright 1985 • Broadman Press

All Rights Reserved

4279-10

ISBN: 0-8054-7910-4

Dewey Decimal Classification Number: 808

Subject Headings: AUTHORSHIP // CHURCH LITERATURE //
PERIODICALS

Library of Congress Catalog Number: 84-23025

Printed in the United States of America

Unless otherwise stated, all Scripture quotations are from the King James Version of
the Bible. Scripture quotations marked TLB are from *The Living Bible.* Copyright ©
Tyndale House Publishers, Wheaton, Illinois, 1971. Used by permission.

Library of Congress Cataloging in Publication Data

Ricks, Chip.
    How to write for Christian magazines.

    Includes index.
    1. Christian literature—Authorship.   I. Marsh,
Marilyn.   II. Title.
BR44.R53   1985   808'.0662   84-23025
ISBN 0-8054-7910-4 (pbk.)

Contents

Foreword by Norman B. Rohrer

Preface

1. Test Your Motive 11

2. Study the Market 17

3. Start the Process 27

4. Gather Some Information 39

5. Organize Your Material 53

6. Make Contact at the Beginning 64

7. Reinforce at the End 77

8. Put It All Together 84

9. Smooth Out the Rough 90

10. Submit 99

Articles 102

    Jean Barnum
    Where the River Jordan Flows 103

    Dave Bourne
    Ken Tada: Lessons in Love 109

    Janet Bollinger
    I Remember the Great San Francisco Earthquake 119

    Timothy N. Boyd
    The Age of Twelve 123

    Carol C. Crawford
    Reach Out and Write Someone 127

    Tim Cummings
    Death Valley Quiet Times 133

    Carol M. Dettoni
    *Changing Their World: An Interview with Tony
    and Lois Evans* 141

    Bruce C. Dodd, Jr.
    How to Quarterback Your Own Education 147

Donnie Galloway
  Nowhere Else to Go 151

Lin Grensing
  The Little Things You May Not Hear 155

Maxine Hancock
  The Child Set in Our Midst 161

Linda Harris
  Are You a Workaholic? 169

Dick Heinlen, as told to Norma West
  Elizabeth's Return 177

Bruce Hekman
  To Wake a Meaning 181

Wayne Jacobsen
  Gethsemane: A Battle Won . . . a Battle Lost 185

Dean Merrill
  The Making of a Slowpoke 191

Charles Mylander
  Sorrow's End 197

Chip Ricks
  100 Years of Compassion 205
  The Lights of Hanukkah Shine on Christmas 211

Ann Thompson
  Family Meetings 217

Albert L. Truesdale
  Christians Living in a Non-Christian World 223

Terry Valley
  God of the Galaxies, Lord of the Leptons 229

Walter Wangerin, Jr.
  The Making of a Minister 233

C. Ellen Watts
  House With a View 241

Sherwood Wirt
  John Calvin: The Burning Heart 247

Foreword

Most fledgling writers cling to the illusion that all crafts require practice, hard work, and confining hours of focused attention—except writing. Consequently, their manuscripts often miss the mark.

This book is disillusioning, and that's good. It provides the proper orientation for people who have thoughts, discoveries, experiences, and insights to share through the printed page.

Chip Ricks and Marilyn Marsh inspire and guide in a most appropriate format. They combine theory with actuality, and there is no better combination for instruction.

How to Write for Christian Magazines is basic editorial vanilla, seasoned with sweet reasonableness. The authors' editorial achievements fit them well for their roles as teachers and authenticate their postulations.

Writing for *Christian* magazines should be only a first step. While believers need the kind of articles, stories, poems and fillers which their fellow pilgrims can prepare, so does the larger reader audience of unbelievers. It is my prayer that writers for the Kingdom of God will also become editorial salt shakers in the secular market as well.

Each year I read hundreds of manuscripts prepared by beginning writers. I shall recommend this book as a first step toward success in feeding the hungry presses which are covering the world with blizzards of literature from Greenland's icy mountains to India's coral strands.

Accept our praise, O Lord, for all your glorious power. We will write . . . to celebrate your mighty acts
— Psalm 21:13 (TLB).

Norman B. Rohrer, Director
Christian Writers Guild

Preface

There are two kinds of writers: those who develop their talents and those who waste them. Study and hard work make the difference. We believe in both. Remember the advice Paul gave to Timothy? "Study to shew thyself approved unto God, a workman that needeth not to be ashamed" (2 Tim. 2:15).

The talent for writing is a gift from God, and no Christian should attempt to write without first seeking the guidance of the Holy Spirit. But the story Jesus told about the man who gave five talents to one servant, two to another, and one to another should be enough to convince us that we are expected to work —work hard—to increase the value of our talents. (Read the story for yourself in Matt. 25:14-30).

Editors of Christian publications are searching for writers who can take an idea, develop it with clear, relevant examples, and leave the reader with a truth which will change his or her life. Yet, poorly written manuscripts continue to flood the desks of editors throughout the country. Most of these manuscripts find their way back to the writers with little indication of what is wrong.

After many years of teaching writing to hundreds of students, we're convinced that almost anyone with a minimum skill in the use of words and a dedication to the task can learn

to write well. And Christian writers can use their talents to serve God. This book, then, is designed for a threefold purpose:
—to explain by example the techniques commonly used by writers of clear, interesting prose.
—to help you step-by-step through the process of writing articles, beginning to end.
—to assist you in getting your work into print.

We asked the editors of twenty-five Christian magazines to select articles which they considered to be excellent models of one type of article regularly published in their magazine. Some editors found it difficult to choose and sent us two or three. We made the final selection. In a few cases we asked permission to use articles which we chose ourselves to demonstrate specific writing techniques. The articles are printed in the back of this book, worded exactly as they originally appeared in the magazines, and all of our illustrations are taken from them. Not only does this provide you with a group of excellent models to study, but you can easily see each illustration in context.

There are hundreds of Christian magazines on the market today. We have purposely chosen twenty-five magazines which give our collection a wide range in content, audience, and writing style.

We encourage you to invest some time to develop your skill; work hard, and you are sure to double your talents.

Chip Ricks
Marilyn Marsh

1

Test Your Motive

Lord, make what I write speak to the hearts of people about Jesus.

—Dr. Robert Walker, Editor, *Christian Life*

The auditorium was quiet as Dr. Robert Walker, editor of *Christian Life* and author of hundreds of articles, paused in his morning address. Three hundred men and women—some published writers, most hope-to-be-published writers, who had gathered for the conference—sat in silence. Dr. Walker was forcing us to reconsider our motive for wanting to write.

Was it for money? for honor and recognition? for fun? Would we write if the reward for thousands of hours of researching, struggling with ideas, typing—typing—typing produced none of these? Would we write if only because we had a burning desire to tell people about Jesus? To tell them what He had done in our lives and the lives of others?

Dr. Walker bowed his head. "Lord," he prayed, "make what I write speak to the hearts of people about Jesus."

Contrast this motive with that of Samuel Johnson who said, "Sir, no man but a blockhead ever wrote except for money." Examine the motive of Nathaniel Hawthorne who wrote, "The only sensible ends of literature are, first, the pleasurable toil of writing; second, the gratification of one's family and friends; and lastly, the solid cash. And not necessarily in that order."

Accomplished secular and Christian writers share many things: dedication to the task, writing techniques, tools of the trade. But their primary motives seldom coincide.

11

What does it take to be a good Christian writer—one whose primary motive for writing is to "speak to the hearts of people about Jesus?" We believe there are six basic requirements.

1. *Be committed to Jesus Christ.* Nothing will substitute—not teachers, not talent, not the best word processor or a set of Bible commentaries. Let's not kid ourselves. If Jesus Christ does not have first priority in our lives, we can't write with firm conviction for Christian periodicals. If the Holy Spirit is to use our writing, we must come to Jesus with willing hearts and open minds.

2. *Be interested in people.* Any good writer is inquisitive. He wants to know why a couple chose to have a dozen children in an age of population explosion. He wants to know why one football team consistently wins and another consistently loses. He wants to know why the suicide rate among young people is so high. Morley Callaghan identified this trait when he said of the writer, "He is always watching. It's a kind of trick of mind."

But just being inquisitive or watchful isn't enough for the Christian writer. He must have a sincere interest in people, an interest that springs from a deep love, a caring about what happens in their lives. Good writing has emotional impact which originates in the heart of the writer, is embedded in his words, and is transmitted to the heart of the reader.

We are by nature far more interested in ourselves than in others. But Jesus was interested in everyone He met. Reread the story of His visit with the Samaritan woman at the well in John 4:5-42. Notice how sensitive Jesus was to her needs, how kind and loving. His interview brought wholeness and produced a beautiful story. The disciples were away taking care of their own needs and missed seeing this life-changing transaction. We learn about the people who surrounded Jesus only because of His interest in them—the leper, the blind man, Mary and Martha, Nicodemus, Jairus, the disciples themselves.

3. *Know your message.* Much of your writing will be for a Christian audience. But thousands of people who are not Christians read Christian periodicals every year. Regardless, the Christian writer must know how to communicate the basic gospel message. Paul called it the "power of God unto salvation to everyone that believeth" (Rom. 1:16). If we believe this, it will come through in our writing.

Three excellent books in this area are Leighton Ford's *Good News,* Howard Hendricks' *Say It with Love,* and Paul Little's *Know Why You Believe.* The Bible, of course, is our primary textbook. The more we study it, the better we will be able to "speak to the hearts of people about Jesus."

4. *Be willing to tithe your time.* Thousands of people are willing to give money for religious or charitable purposes. But few are willing to give their time in an overflowing measure for the pure joy of sharing the love of Jesus. Time is life. As writers we must decide how much time we are willing to give.

Graham Pulkingham, eminent theologian and writer, stretches this idea of tithing even further by suggesting that we are to *be* God's tithe. We are God's "first fruits." The implications of this for the writer's time are profound.

Writing requires time with people: listening, talking, learning, sharing, helping. No writer who shuts himself in a room with a typewriter day after day can be effective for very long.

Writing requires time to read. Keeping abreast of the Christian field is essential, but neither can we neglect the secular field. The basic concerns of persons are mirrored in the daily newspaper, and serious writers of secular literature are often very sensitive to the hurts and emptiness of the human heart. We must read what others are writing—both secular and Christian.

Writing requires time to master the craft. We are God's representatives; we are on His staff. This means that we must strive for excellence. Not only do we have a "huge crowd of men of faith watching us from the grandstands," but we also have numerous critics in the marketplace reviewing our work. The comment "God told me to write this" is the mark of a lazy Christian who is unwilling to take the time to master the craft of writing.

Writing requires a large block of time for writing itself. Ephesians 5:16 speaks of "redeeming the time." *The Living Bible* paraphrases this as "make the most of every opportunity you have." It is common knowledge that we manage to find the time to do those things we really want to do. If we want to write, we will find the time.

5. *Be honest.* There is no room in the Christian writing field for dishonesty. The editor of a leading publishing house recently told us that he would never accept a book for publication before visiting the author in his home. "His life must be consistent with what he writes," he said. "He must be honest to the core."

Rotary International has a motto called the "Four-Way Test" which every Rotarian must apply to his business practices. The four questions can be used equally well to test each article we write: (1) Is it the truth? (2) Is it fair to all concerned? (3) Will it build good will and better friendships? (4) Will it be beneficial to all concerned?

6. *Get a vision of what God can do with your writing.* Mildred Tengbaum and her husband, Luverne, served as missionaries in India for many years. When conditions there forced them to return to the states, Millie was discouraged. "Why did this happen," she asked, "just when our ministry was becoming fruitful?" The Tengbaums had reached many Indians with the message of Christ within the hundred square miles in which they worked. But within a short time, Millie began to get a vision of what God could do with her words if she put them on paper. Today she writes for many leading periodicals. Her arti-

cles in *Moody Monthly* reach an audience of 600,000, in *Scope* an audience of 650,000, and in the *Lutheran Standard* an audience of more than a million people—assuming that only two people read each magazine.

Are you beginning to get the picture?

If you can find yourself somewhere within the range of these six requirements, get ready for an exciting adventure. Being on God's writing staff is not just an ordinary job. You'll be living on the growing edge of your life—an exciting place to be.

Expect to broaden your horizon. Our message is *Jesus.* Can we write about a loving God without learning more about Him? In one of her books Catherine Marshall speaks of the adventure of "spiritual research." The dedicated Christian writer has a lot of one-to-one conversations with God, exploring, searching, researching ideas. She learns more about God and more about herself.

Expect to stretch your understanding. In his book *Language in Thought and Action* S. I. Hayakawa wrote: "To have read *Gulliver's Travels* is to have had the experience, with Jonathan Swift, of turning sick at one's stomach at the conduct of the human race; to read *Huckleberry Finn* is to feel what it is like to drift down the Mississippi River on a raft." Can you imagine how Martha felt when she learned that Jesus was coming to dinner, and she had no food prepared? And can you sense her irritation with Mary who sat listening to her guest rather than helping in the kitchen? Reading can help us relate sensitively to others. This is a real bonus for the writer.

Expect to receive a priceless education. The writer learns as he researches. Did you know that the Salvation Army is a church? That our country first gave official status to military chaplains in 1775? That the Pharisees could probably trace their origin back to the prophet Ezra? We didn't—until research for articles turned up these facts.

Expect to travel if you wish. Travel can broaden your horizon if you view every trip outside your home as an opportunity for an article. Many writers pay vacation expenses by writing about what they have observed, experienced, heard, and learned while traveling. Some established writers travel all over the world on assignments from editors—all expenses paid.

Expect God to give you joy in your writing, whether you write at home in the corner of your bedroom or in the Hilton Hotel on assignment in New York. Paul wrote many of his letters from a prison cell. Yet, he wrote to the Philippians, "I joy, and rejoice with you all" (Phil. 2:17). Later in the same letter, as if the joy of writing to them was almost too much for him, he said, "I have all, and abound: I am full" (4:18).

This joy for the Christian writer has not changed. Sherwood Wirt once wrote, "Give me food and sleep and exercise, and put me in a room by myself with an electric typewriter, a Bible, some dictionaries, a synonym finder, and an idea, and for three hours I wouldn't trade places with anyone on earth."

When you join God's writing staff, you also join the host of Christian writers who down through the ages have shared the love of Jesus with millions. What you write can speak to the hearts of people about Jesus.

2
Study the Market

Editors say it so often they could mumble it in their sleep: study the market.

— Joyce Verrett, Author

One editor estimates that 75 percent of all manuscripts dropped into the mail daily are addressed to the wrong publisher. A missionary article going to *Home Life* magazine, a criticism of child discipline going to *His,* a 3,000-word article on the Psalms going to *Guideposts,* or a 2,000-word article on mass evangelism going to *Today's Christian Woman* are almost certain to be rejected.

But *Home Life* editors are searching for articles on family financial management, husband-wife relationships, and family recreation. *His,* a magazine for college students, needs articles about Christian growth, evangelism and discipleship, with emphasis on practical application. *Guideposts* considers first-person stories of no more than 1,500 words covering one specific incident. And *Today's Christian Woman* welcomes articles targeted to the needs of women, 1,000 to 1,500 words in length.

Professional writers study the market and drastically reduce their rejection slips—and postage. *Writer's Market* lists contact information for 4,000 editors—sales tips directly from those who will buy your words. Obviously, you can't study all of these. Neither would your interests cover the total market. Your objective is to find ten or twelve magazines whose editorial interests coincide with your own, to study them carefully, and to submit your work to the proper market.

Let us suggest a workable plan to help you accomplish this objective.

Collect Sample Magazines and Guidelines

Most authors write best about things which interest them. If you have been reading *Christian Life* for a number of years, you probably like the subject matter, style of writing, length of articles. Wouldn't you like to write for the magazine yourself? Get a few copies ready for study.

Or, if you have discovered that *Living with Children* has given you genuine insight into family relationships, perhaps you would enjoy sharing some of your own experiences with other readers. Gather some issues.

Collect back copies of all the magazines you enjoy reading first—from your own home, from your friends, from your church. Don't hesitate to ask for help. When others discover you are interested in writing, your magazine collection will grow.

Inevitably, you will move from familiar magazines to unfamiliar ones. Visit other churches in your community and ask for surplus copies of denominational magazines. Some book stores carry Christian magazines. Purchase copies of those you want to study.

At this point you should either buy a copy of *Writer's Market* or use one in the library. Updated yearly, the 950 pages of this book are invaluable to the writer. Magazines designed for an audience of professional religious workers are listed in the trade journals section, and religious magazines for children and teenagers will be found in juvenile, teen, and young adult sections.

For the writer interested primarily in writing articles for the general adult audience, the section titled religious, under consumer publications, lists 116 magazines and their writing requirements. Other Christian magazines are listed under their subjects. For example, *Christian Broadcasting Network* appears under the section titled screenwriting; *Church Administration* is found under church administration and ministry; *The Church Musician* is in the music section. Note the kind of information given on *Mature Living,* a popular magazine for senior adults found in the retirement section:

MATURE LIVING, The Sunday School Board of the Southern Baptist Convention, 127 9th Ave. N., Nashville TN 37234. (615)251-2274. Editor: Jack Gulledge. Assistant Editor: Zada Malugen. A Christian magazine for retired senior adults 60+. Monthly magazine; 52 pages. Pays on acceptance. Buys all rights. By-line given. Submit seasonal/holiday material at least 12-15 months in advance. SASE. Reports in 6 weeks. Free sample copy and writer's guidelines.

Nonfiction: How-to (easy, inexpensive craft articles made from easily obtained materials); informational (safety, consumer fraud, labor-saving and money-saving for senior adults); inspirational (short paragraphs with subject matter appealing to older persons); nostalgia; unique personal experiences; and travel. Buys 7-8 mss/issue. Send complete ms. Length: prefers 450 or 925 words; in some cases 1550 words is acceptable for exceptional copy. Pays $14-49.

Photos: Some original photos purchased with accompanying ms. Pays about $5-15 depending on size, b&w glossy prints. Model release required.

Fiction: Everyday living, humor, and religious. "Must have suspense and character interaction." Buys 1 ms/issue. Send complete ms. Length: 925 or 1550 words. Pays 4 cents/word. Short humor, religious or grandparent/grandchild episodes. Length: 125 words maximum. Pays $5.

Tips: "We want warm, creative, unique manuscripts. Presentations don't have to be moralistic or religious, but must reflect Christian standards. Don't write down to target audience. Speak to senior adults on issues that interest them. They like contemporary, good-Samaritan, and nostalgia articles. We buy some light humor. We use 140-word profiles of interesting unusual, senior adults worthy of recognition, when accompanied by a quality action b/w photo. Pays $25. Query should emphasize the uniqueness of proposed copy. Study back issues and guidelines, research and come up with creative material, that hits a need. Rewrite and refine to proper word count."

Later, to place your manuscript properly, you will need the names of editors, addresses, payment for articles, and other information which *Writer's Market* lists.

Now, however, just read through the pages on religious markets and select those magazines you would like to examine. Jot down the titles and addresses. Next write a short letter to the circulation department of each requesting a sample copy of the publication. Be sure to enclose a dollar or two for the magazine, handling, and postage, unless you read that free sample copies are offered to writers.

In the same letter ask for the editor's guidelines for writers. While much information is given in *Writer's Market,* more detailed instructions are often available on request. Some magazines, for example, are developed around a yearly theme. Editorial guidelines prepared for writers state an area of emphasis for each month, give a copy deadline for each issue, and provide a lengthy discussion of the magazine's slant.

Along with other information, *Home Life's* guidelines tell how manuscripts are evaluated:

We screen free-lance material by asking several basic questions about each article: (1) Does it have a Christian message? (2) Does it deal with a family life theme? (3) Is it drawn from the writer's own experience? (4) Is it realistic and true-to-life? (5) Is the writer fair in admitting that his experience might not be the answer for someone else? (6) Does the article have a unique and fresh approach?

Editorial guidelines are well worth the postage and time necessary to obtain them.

Examine Writers' Magazines

While waiting for sample copies of magazines and guidelines to arrive, spend some time reading back and current issues of *Writer's Digest* and *The Writer*. Both magazines may be found in public and college libraries. These monthly periodicals cover the entire publishing field, including the religious market. Their updates on new magazines, address changes of current magazines, changes in editorial staffs and policies, and specific needs of periodicals can save you time and contribute to your effectiveness as a writer.

Many pages of *Writer's Digest* and *The Writer* are devoted to articles of advice—written by writers for writers. This past year articles have appeared on how to write for pure joy, how to write with a specific length in mind, what questions to ask when buying a word processor, and ways to conquer writer's block, for example. Occasionally someone writes about 101 good ideas for articles. And ever so often, these magazines devote almost an entire issue to the religious market.

Study Selected Magazines

With a loose-leaf notebook, paper and pen, sit down with the stack of magazines you have collected and begin your survey. If you own a copy of *Writer's Market*, don't duplicate information in your notebook. If you do not have easy access to this guide, the information you record should be more extensive. Using separate pages for each magazine allows additional sheets of information to be inserted later.

Let's examine a copy of *Family Life Today*. A short column by Clif Cartland, the publisher and editor-in-chief, exudes warmth. He shares three experiences from his day which, he

writes, "lifted my spirits and gave me a new sense of hope."
Two of his experiences involved staff members of the magazine
who expressed concern for him. We sense that the staff is a
family, and supports the philosophical purpose of the magazine
clearly stated in the words below the title on the opposite page:
"Building strong marriages, equipping the Christian home."

Other information on these two pages includes a list of the
editorial staff, address of the magazine, cost of subscription, and
a note to writers: "Manuscripts, art and photographs FLT
welcomes but cannot be responsible for unsolicited material.
Publisher returns only material accompanied by self-addressed
envelope and return postage."

The contents page lists nine articles. A study of these shows
two are short pieces, one approximately 400 words, the other
800 words in length. The shorter piece lists ten ways to revive
family devotions; the other is written by a contributing editor
as an introduction to a cluster of articles on family devotions.
The seven longer articles range in length from 1000 to 2000
words each. Two of these are in the "devotional cluster," one
is an interview, and four concern problems of practical Christian living.

Length of an article is estimated by counting a 100-word
section, and then multiplying by the approximate number of
sections in the article. Or, average the words counted in three
lines, and then multiply by the number of lines in each column.

A few lines about the author found at the end of each article
reveals that all but one of the articles in this issue of *Family Life
Today* were written by free-lance writers. Could you have written the articles? Would you enjoy writing for this magazine? If
so, read a number of issues cover to cover to get a feel for the
writing style, tone, and vocabulary. Jot down any further reaction to the magazine you may have.

Try another example: *His.* Information on the inside cover

states that this magazine is published monthly (October through June) "for the campuses of North America by Inter-Varsity Christian Fellowship." Manuscripts are welcome but "should be accompanied by self-addressed envelope and return postage." The editorial staff is listed and a statement that *"His* is not the official 'last word' on any subject it treats in its brief space. Nor does it state Inter-Varsity Christian Fellowship's official stand on a matter. It is intended to be a mind-stretcher which will help the reader formulate a truly authentic and reasoned biblical faith and lifestyle."

The contents page lists ten entries: nine articles and a poem. Seven of the articles have to do with work or money, one the local church, and one with self-worth. Length of the articles extends from around 400 words to 3,000 words. Three are in the 2,000 to 3,000-word range; two are 1400 to 1600 words; three are 900 to 1000 words; one is a short piece of 400 words. Notes on authors appearing at the end of the articles indicates heavy reliance on free-lance writers.

Like *Family Life Today* and *His,* each magazine you have collected should be carefully studied and data recorded in your notebook.

As you continue to survey magazines, you may begin to note that certain types of articles appear frequently. While combinations and variations of types abound, some attempt at classification may prove helpful—particularly for the beginning writer. We suggest these:

1. *How-to . . .*

This article focuses on how-to-do-something or how-something-was-done. The purpose is to explain a process clearly, one step at a time, so that the reader may do the same thing. In her article, "Reach Out and Write Someone," Carol Crawford shows her readers how they may develop the gift of letter writing. In "To Wake a Meaning" author Bruce Hekman tells his readers how to get children interested in books. In "Family Meetings," Ann Thompson gives a specific example of a meeting with her own family and then guides her readers step by step in setting up their own. Among the many magazines that welcome how-to articles are *Family Life Today, Today's Christian Woman,* and *Light and Life.*

2. *Report*

A report article conveys information—facts, figures, quotes. The purpose is to explain, to inform. "Where the River Jordan Flows" by Jean Barnum and "The Age of Twelve" by Timothy Boyd are both reports. Often a report has an underlying purpose of changing a reader's mind or actions. When the reader has all the information, the writer hopes he will respond, act, or think differently. The article may begin with the presentation of a problem supported by verifiable research and close with a suggested solution. "Christian Living in a Non-Christian World" by Albert L. Truesdale is a good example of this type of report. *Eternity, Moody Monthly,* and *Christian Life,* all contain examples of report articles.

3. *Narrative*

This type of article may be either personal or biographical. The personal narrative shares the writer's experience from the first person point of view. The biographical narrative involves the reader in an experience from a third-person point of view. The subject may be someone living or dead. While facts are important in all narratives, they don't override the story which generally follows a dramatic lead in chronological order. Three narrative articles for your study are "House with a View" by Ellen Watts, "Elizabeth's Return" by Dick Heinlen and Norma West, and "The Making of a Slowpoke" by Dean Merrill. *Live* and *Guideposts* offer good examples of personal narratives while *Biblical Illustrator* and *Sunday Digest* often publish biographical narratives.

4. *Profile*

Focus of the profile article is either on an individual or an organization. The writer's purpose is to bring a character or organization to life on paper—to paint word pictures for the reader. Direct quotes, vivid descriptions, and interesting anecdotes are all part of the profile article. Individuals are profiled in Janet Bollinger's article, "I Remember the Great San Francisco Earthquake," and Sherwood Wirt's "John Calvin: The Burning Heart." An organization is profiled in "100 Years of Compassion." *Readers Digest* has used profiles for years. Religious magazines such as *Charisma, Worldwide Challenge, Christian Herald,* and *Sunday Digest* include this type in almost every issue.

5. *Interview*

Emphasis in this type of article is on what the individual being interviewed says—his ideas, his opinions. Although the major part of the content is supplied by the interviewee, the writer may add some biographical data or other carefully researched facts. The two interviews included as examples of this type of article are Dave Bourne's "Ken Tada: Lessons in Love," and Carol Dettoni's " Changing Their World: An Interview with Tony and Lois Evans." *Family Life Today, Christian Herald,* and *Christianity Today,* among other Christian magazines, publish interviews.

6. *Inspirational*

This article leads the reader through spiritual reflections on some problem, belief, or Scripture truth. The purpose is to lift the reader, to help her gain deeper insight. "Death Valley Quiet Times" by Tim Cummings, "Gethsemane: A Battle Won, A Battle Lost" by Wayne Jacobsen, and " God of the Galaxies, Lord of the Leptons" by Terry Valley, are all inspirational articles. *His, Herald of Holiness,* and *Seek* are three of the many magazines that use this type.

Many magazines use all of these types of articles. Other magazines use three or four. It is the writer's responsibility to know the types of articles editors need.

Limit Your Market

From the magazines you have surveyed, select ten or twelve you believe most nearly meet your needs as a person and as a writer. Determine now to read each of them every month, becoming more and more familiar with your personal market.

If you decide to subscribe to the magazines, you will soon need a method of storage. Plastic or fiberboard file boxes which hold a year's supply of magazines and fit nicely on bookshelves serve this purpose well. Your local office supply store may carry these. Whatever method of storage you select, be sure the magazines are handy for reference and research.

Magazines which interest you but do not make the top ten can be treated differently. We keep only a sample copy of each.

Eventually you may want to set up a vertical file, labeling a manila folder with the title of each magazine on your limited and extended prospective market list. In each folder you can place all correspondence with the editor, guidelines, a sample of the magazine, and copies of submitted manuscripts.

A survey of the writing market is never complete. New magazines appear; old ones sometimes fold. An editor moves on to other challenges, and the style of a magazine and its editorial needs change. On one magazine more staff are hired, and fewer free-lance articles are accepted. On another, format expansion brings no additions to staff, and more free-lance articles are needed.

Good writers must keep in touch, be alert to changes, and continually study the market.

3

Start the Process

The vitality of thought is in adventure. Ideas won't keep.
Something must be done about them.
—Alfred North Whitehead, American philosopher (1861-1947)

Did the market survey cram your head with dozens of writing ideas? Sometimes a picture, an advertisement, or a couple of words glaring from the printed page will generate an idea for an article—and generate enthusiasm for writing it. At other times, however, surveying what others have written brings frustration: "It must have taken weeks for Lloyd Ogilvie to write that article. Where can I find that kind of time?"

We don't know Lloyd Ogilvie personally, but he is pastor of one of the largest churches in Hollywood, California, a popular television Bible teacher, and a prolific writer. We suspect that he settled the practical problems of writing a long time ago.

And so must you—even before you begin to deal with the ideas you're anxious to get on paper.

Settling the Practical Problems

Let's consider three questions: (1) Where can you work? (2) When can you work? (3) What materials do you need?

Finding a quiet place away from eager children or a busy telephone often presents a challenge. If an entire room in your home is available, fine. If not, be imaginative. How about a corner of the bedroom? a space in the dining room? one side of the garage?

If working at home causes problems, early arrival at the

library will give you squatter's rights to choice tables. John Updike turned out a whole book in a small-town library. Or, investigate the possibility of using space at your local church. During the week many rooms go unused—quiet spacious rooms with large tables for spreading your materials.

When you have found your "writer's studio," check your daily schedule and determine that you will set aside certain hours every day for writing. Even the person with an eight-hour-a-day job can free an early morning or evening hour if writing is a priority.

With place and time settled, gather some writing materials. Paper and pen are the only two essentials, but few editors today will accept handwritten manuscripts. The following checklist will give you a start toward getting your workshop in order.

1. Typewriter
2. Number two pencils, pens
3. Lined tablets (unless you compose on the typewriter or word processor)
4. Second sheets (for typed rough drafts)
5. Carbon second sheets (unless you use a copy machine)
6. Twenty-pound weight bond paper (for final copies)
7. Cellophane tape
8. Paper clips
9. Envelopes: 4 by 9 1/2 and 10 by 12
10. Stamps
11. Dictionary
12. Thesaurus

Be sure your Bible and magazine collection are close at hand. Other reference books helpful to anyone writing for religious periodicals are Bible commentaries, dictionaries, concordances, handbooks, histories, and Old and New Testament surveys.

With practical concerns settled, we are ready to deal with ideas.

Generating Ideas

Begin with yourself.

What are your current and past interests? experiences? achievements? problems? Make a list.

The list of a friend of ours included items such as music, history, plants, boating, water skiing, travel, reading, mission work, campus ministries, wife, mother, Sunday School teacher, church visitation committee, an ill parent, a challenging son. Her list went on and on.

So will yours. And the list can be productive. With a little research, the information stored in your head can be shaped into articles which interest and help other people. Lists help the writer to retrieve information. For example, suppose "Sunday School teacher" is on your list. What unique ideas have you used in teaching your students which you could share with other teachers? How have you solved discipline problems? What have you learned from your students? Is there a particular student who would make interesting subject material? Have you entertained them in your home? Visited their families? All of these questions could lead to articles.

Mark Staples, features editor of *The Lutheran,* said, "Many writers don't ask 'What does my writing have to offer the average reader out there? How can it change someone's life because of what I have learned or because of what happened to me or someone else?' " These are important questions. Ask them.

When you have completed your personal list, don't stop. Keep going with the people you know. Does your brother-in-law write church music? There's an article idea. Put it on a list. Is your father having difficulty adjusting to retirement? There's an article idea. Has your neighbor invited you to join a Bible study group or a friend changed church affiliations? Two more ideas.

Once you've gotten into the list-making habit, extend it to include the ideas that come to you in the course of a day as you drive to work, do the washing, attend committee meetings, or read the daily newspaper. In addition to examining yourself and others for ideas, you must read, listen, and observe.

Read, listen, observe.

Numerous articles and books have come from a writer's noticing a particular newspaper story. Theodore Dreiser, for instance, got the idea for his *An American Tragedy* from a newspaper item. Stories of people and events fill the daily newspaper. If you read it carefully, you will find good things as well as bad. Clip any item which triggers an idea, identify it with date and source, and file it along with your lists.

Some writers make a weekly practice of going to the library just to browse. Most are avid readers; in particular they read what others in the same market are writing. During the past year, for instance, articles have appeared on overcoming depression, worry, helping disabled children, failure in the ministry, handling criticism, mother and daughter relationships, spiritual revivals, telling others about Christ, handling the future. Other articles have been published on Christian music, world hunger, local churches moving into television, biking, complaining, the healing power of forgiveness, parents in revolt, lessons in faith, the legality of military chaplains, pornography, hospitality, and stepchildren.

These are only a sampling of subjects on which hundreds of articles were written. And they don't begin to touch the interview, personal narrative, and profile articles written on individuals!

In addition to reading, listen when others talk—really listen. When friends discover you're interested in writing, they will feed you all kinds of ideas and information. Train yourself to observe carefully what goes on around you. What are people doing? And why? Note facial expressions, mannerisms, movements.

Generating ideas is an ability which can be learned, cultivated, and expanded. Once you've acquired a special sense of alertness, you will never lack for writing ideas. They will come without conscious effort.

Moving Ahead

Test the idea.

Shaping a general idea into a finished article involves several important steps. First, give any idea you're considering a close scrutiny. Is your interest in it intense? Intense enough to spend considerable time on it? Would anyone else be interested? Interested enough to read about it? Who? Be precise as you can. Would it be helpful to them? How? Is your idea timely but not restrictively so? That is, would a reader enjoy knowing about a particular evangelistic crusade six months from now as well as now? Or does a current event lend itself to Christian interpretation? Can you get the information needed to develop the idea into a story? Can you obtain the interviews or locate the information close at hand? Would you be able to travel for it? Finally, has the idea been used before? If a check of periodical indexes and a review of Christian magazines indicates that it has, can you come up with a variation?

At this point, if you still feel the subject is a viable one, gather enough information to give you a good overview of the general subject area. For example, suppose you are interested in writing an article on unemployment. Your preliminary check for information turned up a dozen articles listed in *Readers' Guide to Periodical Literature,* at least three in Christian periodicals. Read two or three of the articles. Talk to an unemployed friend.

Visit the state employment office. If you have been unemployed, jot down some notes about the problems you experienced, the lessons you learned.

A few hours of this preparatory research should glean enough information to help you decide what facet of unemployment interests you most. Sit down, read through your notes, and think. Do you want to examine the emotional trauma involved? How God can help in this time of stress? A personal narrative, interview, or an inspirational article might be appropriate. Do you want to find out how many people experience unemployment? What churches are doing to help? A report might be best. Are you interested in an individual who finds jobs for senior citizens? Or an organization? A profile would be in order. Could you lead someone through the steps of finding a good job? That's an idea for a how-to article.

Determine the focus.

To shape your writing idea into article form, you need to determine your main intention—the major idea on which all other ideas in your article are brought to bear. What exactly do you want your reader to learn from reading your article? The answer to this question will determine the focus of your writing —the angle of vision. As this focus guides every word you write, you must decide specifically enough that you can express it as one sharp idea. "I want to convey something about prayer" is far too general. Try: "Joy and peace are the by-products of daily prayer." Expressed that clearly, both you and your reader know what direction you're taking as you move through your article.

Let's go back to the unemployment idea. Your focus might be, "I wasn't prepared for unemployment, but, like Peter, I learned to rejoice in the midst of trials," a personal experience story. Or it might be, "Unemployment is a problem of the Christian church," a report showing the large number of Christians facing this problem and what the church can do to help.

"Senior citizens are producing" might profile an organization developed to assist the unemployed elderly and encourage readers to help in similar ways. "Most of us will be jobless at least once in our lives, and this can be a time for Christian growth" was the focus chosen by Joyce E. Coe for her article "How to Be Profitably Unemployed" which appeared in *Christian Herald* in February, 1979.

Bringing a general subject into focus, limiting its range, determining the major point you wish to make, will now make your topic a workable length for a magazine article. You are ready to move ahead with your idea.

Query the editor.

A query is merely a letter asking if an editor is interested in seeing an article on a particular subject. While a fiction writer must submit an entire story, unless he is a famous author, the non-fiction writer can query the editor before writing his article. A query is not necessary for short pieces, of course, as they can often be written in less time than it takes to write a good query. But lengthy research is seldom undertaken by professionals without first locating an interested editor. Some magazines will not accept a manuscript unless a query and an editor's expressed interest precedes it.

For the writer, the query can save time, energy, and money. And writing flows much easier when directed toward a particular magazine. Audience, style, and length, for example, are more easily determined.

The query letter stands as an example of your best writing. Don't dash it off with a few clangs of the typewriter. Spend time roughing it out, getting it into concise, interesting form, checking it for mechanical problems and typing it neatly as a correct business letter.

A good query must:

1. Attract the editor with the first sentence and contain a capsule summary or outline of the idea.

2. Show the editor why he and his readers should care about the subject.

3. State available sources of information.

4. Tell why you are qualified to write the article or offer to write on speculation.

Study the following examples of query letters which produced positive responses from editors.

Example 1

Dear Sir:

When I read that Billy Graham consistently used four or five psalms for his morning devotionals, my interest was pricked. I tried the same pattern, and have discovered the joy of sharing the voice of God's people. Here, from the depths of the human spirit, men praise God and rejoice in his care, weep for their sins and plead for forgiveness, marvel at the greatness of the Creator and fear for his power.

When I began to study the imagery of the psalms (the potter's vessel, wax melting before a fire, a rod of iron, shepherd caring for his sheep), I gained a new appreciation for the poets who could express my feelings so well. Man's most intense emotions are in these psalms: fear, trust, anger, joy, hate, love. Because the Book of Psalms has come to mean so much to me, I would like to share something of what I have learned with your readers.

An article of approximately 1200-1500 words giving something of the history, purpose and moving language of the psalms could enrich the readers' understanding and help them to use the psalms more meaningfully in their lives.

I believe that I am qualified to write the article for you. I have taught an adult Sunday School class for many years,

I teach writing at our local community college, and I have had several articles published in Christian periodicals.

Sincerely,

Example 2

Dear Sir:

Many parents live through the high school years with their teenagers, not really understanding them, and (if they're honest) heaving a sigh of relief when they graduate and leave the nest. But I know an army family who searches for teenagers to live with them. In the past four years, June and Bob Jones have had eighty-eight boys and girls live in their home as part of their family.

Bob, a major in the United States Army, and June, his wife, a five-foot-two blond with sparkling blue eyes, have six children and a golden-haired Pekingese all their own. But when fifteen-year-old Pattie, in trouble with the police, knocked on their door in May and asked if she could live with them, they just couldn't say no. That was the beginning of a steady stream of disturbed teenagers who have found the warm, loving atmosphere of the Jones's home a welcome substitute for the cold discipline of reform schools.

Bob and June have consistently refused government aid because they want to be free to accept any teenager who comes to them for help. The forty loaves of bread weekly, forty gallons of milk, pounds of meat and potatoes, and dozens of boxes of cereal, send their grocery bill soaring to between $700 and $800 monthly. This, added to the clothing, housing, and school expenses for such an extended family could never be met on a major's salary. Yet, they have never failed to pay their monthly bills.

I believe your readers would be interested in knowing

the Jones family, some of their teenagers, and the unique way this family's budget is met. Although I'm not a published writer, I have twenty years of experience as a military wife behind me. And I am willing to write this article for you on speculation.

Sincerely,

Example 3

Dear Sir:

On September 2, 1977, Connie Engel earned her silver wings and became the first woman pilot in the history of the United States Air Force to solo an Air Force jet. At graduation exercises she was awarded three of the four top honors, including the coveted Commander's Trophy, in a class of thirty-six men and ten women.

Many marriages would have crumbled during that year of intensive training with its fourteen-hour days. Not only was Connie struggling with navigation, aerodynamics, and aerobatics, but Rich, her Air Force pilot husband, was undergoing an even more strenuous course for test pilots.

The Engels's marriage held firm. Both Connie and Rich are quick to tell anyone who asks that all their orders come from the Lord. Committed Christians who love Jesus Christ, the Engels are open to any demands He makes on their lives. This openness has led them to fly jets faster than the speed of sound at 40,000 feet in the air, to fix omelets with green peppers and cheese at 3:00 AM for hungry airmen, and to fly to Hawaii to tell a high school group of girls that "God can help you choose exciting careers."

Forty-one percent of the working force in America today is women. This includes many young couples who are struggling with the stress of both husband and wife working.

I believe Connie and Rich's story would help and encourage this group of readers, as well as be of interest to others who may be led to understand that God often has a unique plan for our lives.

I'd like to do an article on the Engels for you, and I could furnish some excellent photographs. Connie is my daughter, and I have a wealth of information to draw on. As a free lance, I have written a number of articles for Christian periodicals; the latest article appears in this month's *Worldwide Challenge.*

Sincerely,

A self-addressed stamped envelope (SASE) should be enclosed with every query letter. When it is dropped in the mail, forget it. Often a reply does not come for four to six weeks.

Don't be discouraged when you receive rejections. All writers receive them—even the best. The editor may not feel your idea is right for his publication for a number of reasons. The subject may have been handled too recently by a competing magazine. The idea may not fit in with other planned articles. Or the editor may have assigned the idea to someone else before your query arrived. If you still feel your idea is good, try another publication.

If the editor likes your idea, but is unfamiliar with your writing, he will probably react in hedged language. For example: "Your idea interests me. If you want to write the article on speculation, I will be happy to read it." Naturally, an editor cannot commit himself until he is sure you can turn out a printable story. Be encouraged that he is interested. You have found a possible market. The rest is up to you.

Occasionally, an editor will phone you if he especially likes an idea and wants the article promptly. When this happens, it is best to follow the telephone conversation with a letter to be sure that no misunderstanding occurs. For example, the query letter on the Engels brought a call from an editor giving precise instructions. This follow-up letter was then sent to him:

Dear Mr. Lee:

It is my understanding from our phone conversation yesterday that you want an article of about 1500 words on Connie and Rich Engel, with an emphasis on their marriage, their reliance on God, problems, and temptations. I plan to include some of the adjustments Connie had to make during flight training and the tests she faced as she entered a man's profession.

Pictures will include the following as you suggested: Connie and Rich in dress uniform, Connie and Rich with the T-38 aircraft, Connie receiving awards, Connie and Rich relaxing at home, Connie as a little girl.

If I have omitted anything, or if you have any further suggestions, let me know. The manuscript will be in your hands by April 1.

Sincerely,

One caution: don't submit query letters until you are sure you can write the articles. A good test is to wait until you have had three or four shorter articles, requiring no query, accepted for publication.

Regardless, your ideas are now in process. You are on your way to becoming a published writer.

4

Gather Some Information

Never sit down at the typewriter until you have your facts. The amateur starts with half-formed ideas and pops off about something he has not thoroughly researched. The professional waits until he has touched all the bases. . . .
—Sherwood Wirt, Author and former Editor of *Decision*

Sherwood Wirt's comment may come as a surprise to you. You may be itching to get your fingers on the typewriter, ready to transfer everything you know from your head onto paper. If so, you may well be asking, "Do I have to do research?" Many beginning writers hit the typewriter sure that they can rely on their memory, charm, and writing style. "All for naught," says *Writer's Digest* editor John Brady, "if you're not, above all, a researcher."

Perhaps you may feel that because your article is to be about yourself, your life, your experiences, that no research is necessary. What difference does it make whose statue stands on the courthouse square in your hometown? Or if Burke's five-and ten-cent store burned in 1940 or 1941? Or if the county sheriff is now Smith or Jones? A lot. No magazine editor wants to print untruths as facts—certainly not in Christian magazines. Somewhere in your hometown somebody knows the truth, and editors do not like to receive embarrassing corrections.

More often, your article idea is not related to your personal experience. This calls for even more checking, more research, more gathering of facts. Readers of today's Christian periodicals are educated and informed. They travel, read, watch the latest news, listen to lectures, attend college classes. Most of the magazines you will be writing for have a readership of more than 100,000 people. These readers not only expect a new slant on your material, they expect up-to-date, accurate information.

While not every editor has time to check all the details, the larger magazines have personnel who do nothing else. We know of no editor who will print an article written by a beginner without doing some checking. And when an error is discovered? You've lost your credibility and your chance for future assignments. Your objective is to build a reputation for accuracy. A good rule of thumb applicable to most articles is two thirds research time and one third writing time.

But where can you find the major religions of the Republic of Seychelles? A T-38 jet aircraft flight manual? The author of *We Do Not Know One Millionth of One Percent About Anything?*

Begin with a Personal Library

You have already assembled a collection of the magazines you are interested in, and as writers are almost always avid readers, you must have a collection of favorite books as well. This is the beginning of your personal library.

Within easy reach, keep several good translations of the Bible (many publishers use only the King James; others prefer later versions), a dictionary, thesaurus, grammar handbook, *Writer's Market,* and a few other reference books that you find yourself using frequently. As you begin to build your personal library, examine reference books at your Bible bookstore. Talk to other Christian writers and find out what books are most helpful to them. Ask for recommendations from your pastor. To start, look over the following list of specialized Bible references which we have found helpful:

Archaeology

Albright, William F. *New Horizons in Biblical Research.* London: Oxford Univ. Press, 1966.

Kitchen, K. A. *The Bible in Its World: The Bible and Archaeology Today.* Madison, Wis.: Inter-Varsity Press, 1978.

Commentaries

The Broadman Bible Commentary. Nashville: Broadman Press, 1969.

Guthrie, D., J. A. Motyer, et al. *The New Bible Commentary: Revised.* Grand Rapids, Mich.: Wm. B. Eerdmans Pub. Co., 1970.

Meyer, F. B. *Bible Commentary.* Wheaton, Ill.: Tyndale House, 1979.

Pfeiffer, Charles F. and Everett F. Harrison. *The Wycliffe Bible Commentary.* Chicago: Moody Press, 1962.

Concordances

Strong, James. *Strong's Exhaustive Concordance of the Bible,* rev. ed. Nashville: Abingdon, 1980.

Young, Robert. *Analytical Concordance to the Bible,* rev. ed. Nashville: Thomas Nelson, 1982.

Geography and Culture

Baly, Denis. *The Geography of the Bible,* rev. ed. New York: Harper and Bros., 1974.

Everyday Life in Bible Times. New York: National Geographic Society, 1976.

Frank, Harry T., ed. *Atlas of the Bible Lands.* Nashville: Broadman Press, 1979.

Great People of the Bible and How They Lived. Pleasantville, N.Y.: Reader's Digest, 1974.

Packer, James I., Merrill C. Tenney and William White, Jr. *The Bible Almanac.* Nashville: Thomas Nelson Pub., 1980.

Histories

Edersheim, Alfred. *Old Testament Bible History.* 1 vol. ed. Grand Rapids, Mich.: Eerdmans Pub. Co., 1982.

Bruce, F. F. *New Testament History.* Garden City, N.Y.: Oliphants and Doubleday, 1971.

Dowley, Tim, John H. Y. Briggs, et al. *Eerdmans' Handbook to the History of Christianity.* Grand Rapids, Mich.: Eerdmans Pub. Co., 1977.

Johnson, Paul. *Civilizations of the Holy Land.* London: Weidenfeld and Nicolson, 1979.

Surveys

Harrison, Everett F. *Introduction to the New Testament,* rev. ed. Grand Rapids, Mich.: Eerdmans Pub. Co., 1964.

Harrison, Ronald Kenneth. *Introduction to the Old Testament.* Grand Rapids, Mich.: Eerdmans Pub. Co., 1969.

Tenney, Merrill C. *New Testament Survey.* Grand Rapids, Mich.: Eerdmans Pub. Co., 1961.

Other works which are nice to have close at hand are anthologies of good literature, religious biographies, and books on writing. As your library grows, you will find a Rolodex, Eldon, or some similar card index file helpful in keeping your books in order for easy reference.

In chapter 3 we urged prospective writers to read, listen, and observe in order to develop article ideas. The same process can generate information as well. By formalizing it a bit, you can make it contribute to your personal library. When you hear a good anecdote or when you learn the name of someone who has had an unusual experience, jot down the facts and place them in a file folder marked "Idea File" or "Anecdotes." Similarly, when you observe something or have a personal experience which moves you, make some notes on that experience and file them. When you read the newspaper, clip any articles of special interest, and drop them in a file folder. As you clip and save, you are developing an information bank. No longer will you rack your brain trying to remember something because you are now establishing easy access to information.

A personal library is not only helpful but a constant means of learning. It does, however, take time to build. And it does cost money. In the meantime, you may have to go outside your home for most of the information you need.

Use Community Resources

The most obvious community resource for the writer is the public library. If you are not familiar with your local library, spend a few hours there browsing, talking to the librarian, perhaps taking a library tour, and learn to use this valuable resource quickly and efficiently.

Most books in the public library may be checked out for specific time periods. Others, such as encyclopedias or yearbooks, are references and must be used at the library. If it is not convenient for you to take notes there, copy machines are standard equipment in most libraries today so that you may reproduce information. In addition to books, libraries carry issues of magazines and newspapers dating back many years. Current issues will be on library shelves; others may be stored in vaults or reproduced on microfilm.

In many libraries material of local interest is assembled in a vertical file. Items such as newspaper clippings, government reports, business brochures, and medical pamphlets are clipped and filed in folders according to subject. Vertical files may also hold collections of government materials. No other printer exceeds the volume of the United States Printing Press. Increasingly, too, libraries offer collections of movies, slides, recordings, and videotapes.

With so much material available, how do you go about determining what you need? Begin with the card catalogue. Every library has this file which is an index to all the books in the library filed alphabetically. In some libraries this file is made up of 3 by 5 cards. In others the file is computerized. In both systems, every book is entered in three ways: by author, title, and subject. Each entry supplies all the information needed to locate the book in the library. By going to the subject file, you can make a list of all the books in the library which have information on your idea.

After you have checked to see what books are available on your subject, work through some of the periodical indexes to find out what has been published in periodicals. While there are indexes to most subject areas, only two of the larger ones limit their entries to religious periodicals. The *Christian Periodical Index* was first published in 1959. It comes out quarterly with an annual cumulation, and a cumulative index every three years. Articles are indexed by subject and author. The *Religion Index One: Periodicals* was first published in 1949. It comes out twice a year with a two-year cumulative index. Entries are by author, subject, and some titles.

Readers' Guide to Periodical Literature is a popular index which has come out annually since 1900. The periodicals indexed are of a general, popular nature, but these are often helpful to the Christian writer. This guide does index a few religious periodicals. The *New York Times Index, Business Index, Education Index,* and *Humanities Index,* among others, are found in most libraries.

Not only do indexes like these help you to locate articles which have been written on your subject, but they help you evaluate marketing potential for your idea as well. If an index tells you that *Christianity Today* published an article on Martin Luther just six months ago, it is doubtful that the editor of this magazine will be looking for another one anytime soon.

A word of wisdom: if you do not know how to use these files and indexes to find library materials, don't waste your time guessing. Ask the librarian for help. A few minutes of expert instruction will save you valuable time and prevent possible mistakes. We have not yet found a librarian who was not willing to offer assistance to writers. A friendly relationship with a competent librarian can become one of your greatest assets. Reference librarians are generally challenged by research questions which stump the beginning writer, and are anxious to help you track down a quotation or obscure fact. Frequently, libraries offer reference services by telephone. The New York City Public Library has a full-time staff of four who will take any question which they can answer with no more than five minutes of research. Inquire about this service at your local library.

While you are in the reference section, you might want to become familiar with the *Hammond Ambassador World Atlas,* an important source of political and physical maps, agriculture, industries, population, foreign flags, currency, and religions. *Atlas of the Biblical World* by Denis Baly and A. D. Tushingham, and the *Pictorial Bible Atlas* edited by E. M. Blaiklock are more specialized.

All writers should be familiar with *Current Biography* and the *Who's Who* series. These contain biographies of various lengths of prominent people, some with portraits. *Who's Who in the Bible,* edited by Albert Sims and George Dent is a quick reference to all biblical personalities.

Don't overlook the dictionaries which offer far more information than pronunciation and definition. The *Oxford English Dictionary* gives the history of words from the date they first entered the language. In the 1728 pages of *Webster's New World*

Dictionary are found 36,000 words in explanatory articles on language in addition to the 159,000 entries. More specialized dictionaries are the *New Bible Dictionary* in a beautiful three volume edition put out by Tyndale House and *Wilson's Dictionary of Bible Types* which is often helpful when a writer is dealing with symbols.

Examine several sets of encyclopedias—the *Americana,* the *Britannica, World Book.* Then look at some of the Bible encyclopedias. *Family Encyclopedia of the Bible* published by Eerdmans is one.

Fact books are often quick sources of information: *Facts on File, The American Book of Days, Information Please Almanac, Kane Book of Famous First Facts and Records, Names and Numbers,* among others.

As you move from shelf to shelf, make notes of the reference materials you believe will be most helpful. Take time now to examine them carefully.

While not all libraries are public, most are available to the writer. College and university libraries, church and synogogue libraries, are excellent resources. City newspapers have libraries —sometimes called morgues. If you are not sure of access to any of these, call and ask. Chances are your request will be granted.

Reach Out to People

While libraries will be your primary community resource, consider others as well: your local chamber of commerce, state department of tourism, and other government offices, schools, agencies and organizations such as Wesley House, Parents Without Partners, the Red Cross, Girls' Club. Remember, too, your local church and its affiliations. The people who work in all these organizations are specialists in their fields, and most often they are happy to share their knowledge and expertise with writers.

Along with this, most organizations have pamphlets which are designed to inform the public about their work. These are free for the asking. Not long ago we were doing some research for a book on child abuse. The materials handed to us from government and private agencies filled a huge box. The people we talked to were grateful for any publicity we could give their cause.

One last comment on people sources: don't overlook the obvious. Your next-door neighbor, close friend, pastor, or cousin may be a library of information on the topic you are researching.

Learn Time-Saving Research Techniques

Locating the information you need, whether in the library or in a human source, is only the beginning. You must know how to limit your research to the information you need and how to retrieve it efficiently. Professional writers follow a research system—their own or somebody else's. Here's a simple system with techniques that work:

Step One: Plot research needs before you begin.

1. Jot down what you already know about your subject. The idea for the article "100 Years of Compassion," for example, came from the comment of a friend as we passed a Christmas kettle: "The Salvation Army will be celebrating its 100th anniversary next year." And that is the first comment on a note card:

100th anniversary in 1980.
Christian organization—preaching salvation.
Always have Christmas kettles.
Have doughnut stations at disasters.

Operate clothing stores.
Brass bands.
Operated USOs in WW2.
Members wear uniforms.

2. Write out a preliminary major idea, or focus, for your subject. This may be changed later, but it will help to guide your research. The preliminary major idea for the Salvation Army article was developed from the notes above: "The Salvation Army has been preaching salvation and ministering to the poor for 100 years."

3. Sketch a tentative outline; break your major idea into sections. Is there a key word in the statement which will help you? The "100 years" in our example idea hints of a chronological approach. Here's the breakdown:

    I. Beginning of the Salvation Army
   II. Growth of the Salvation Army
  III. Salvation Army today

4. Using your preliminary outline, make a list of information you must gather. This list originates from questions you ask yourself. What, specifically, do you want to know? The answer to that question produced this list for the Salvation Army research:

    I. Beginning of the Salvation Army
      How did it begin? Who started it?
      Where was it started? When was it started?
      What was the purpose? What kinds of social and religious work did they do? Note: look for beginning of brass band, Christmas kettle, uniforms.
   II. Growth of the Salvation Army
      Names of leaders? Numbers of people involved?
      Rules? Organization? Where did they expand?

Any problems? Any changes in purpose or organization as they expanded? Note: watch for anecdotes.
III. Salvation Army today
Officers? Pay? Numbers involved?
Organization? Purpose? Religious and social work?
Any government financing?

5. Set up a file folder. Performing this step becomes increasingly important as you become more and more professional. Most well-known writers work on a number of articles at the same time. File folders labeled with article titles will keep information separated and safe.

Step Two: Locate people sources and start the ball rolling.

1. Make phone calls. If there are people you can interview or organizations you need to visit, now is the time to make appointments. Two interviews were set up to gather information for the Salvation Army article. One was with Lt. Bill Flynn at the Divisional Headquarters in Los Angeles; the other was with Lt. Ben Nunes at the local Santa Maria, California, office.

2. Write letters and mail them. If your information is close at hand, you may skip this step. But if the United States government, corporations, or organizations in distant cities can help you (and if you have time to wait for the information), get letters of request on their way.

Step Three: Record information. To be professional in your approach to writing, it is wise to make a complete file of your research activities for every article. This means that you take notes for every book or reference consulted. It means also that you make a note of each phone call, record the name of each person who assists you, and make notes on all interviews. Basically you do all this so that your work will be easy, accurate, and verifiable.

As you gather information for an article, drop it in a file

folder. This may include tear sheets of articles friends hand you, newspaper clippings, bulletins and pamphlets given to you by various sources, notes taken from library materials—anything which will help you in writing the article.

When you take library notes, list the title of the work, the author, publisher, and date. This is standard bibliographical procedure and will make it easier later if you need to check a point or respond to any questions raised by editors or readers. A list of sources with corresponding numbers on your notes is an easy method to follow. Some writers prefer 4 by 5 cards for notes; others prefer half sheets of paper or pages of a loose-leaf notebook. Whatever your choice, be sure you can later shuffle your notes to order them for writing. Sometimes you will want to quote a source directly. Be sure, then, to include the material within quotation marks and to record the page number. More often, you will want to put the information into your own words, rewriting it as succinctly as possible.

As important as library notes are, they are what scholars call "secondary" sources. The interview is often your opportunity to get firsthand information, to get a fresh view, an interesting and original quotation. The notes you take during interviews are vital. If you would like to tape the interview, be sure to request permission. Even then, it is wise to take notes. More than one writer has lost valuable information because of a faulty tape or recorder.

If you are able to have your interview in a quiet, comfortable place, you will have an easier time establishing a friendly rapport. It is your job to win the confidence of the respondent. Since you have already gathered considerable information from library sources, you should be able to ask the right questions. If you are working on an article about the person you are interviewing, you should be as familiar with his background and accomplishments as possible. Usually time for an interview is limited. Don't waste it asking questions you can research in advance.

The questions you do ask are important. Prepare them beforehand. And give extra thought to the preparation of the first question. It sets the tone—shallow, stimulating, warm and caring, or cold. Begin with open-ended questions. These are questions which cannot be answered with one word. Some of those prepared for the interview with Lt. Nunes were these:

1. With your college degree, you could make much more money working for some company. What reasons do you have for staying in the Salvation Army?

2. The rules of the Salvation Army state that members must get permission from their superiors to marry. How did you feel about that?

If you have difficulty forming open-ended questions, try beginning with one of these groups of words: "In what ways . . ." "What are some of the reasons . . ." "What do you see . . ." "What kinds of things . . ." "How do you think . . ." and "How do you feel about . . ."

Closed questions, those requiring only a word or two to answer, can be used as follow-ups for the responses to open-ended questions. For example: Do you plan to run a summer camp for children this year? Here in Santa Maria? Will there be one in Santa Barbara as well?

Most of us would rather talk than listen. But learning to listen during an interview is essential. Be sensitive. Listen for comments that might lead to other vital information. Careful listening can produce a title for your article, a lead, a major idea, an angle, choice anecdotes. The title "100 Years of Compassion" was dropped casually by Lt. Nunes during the interview, and later became part of the major idea of the article.

To close the interview, you might ask, "Is there anything else you would like to say about . . .?" or "Is there anything you would like included that I have overlooked?" Briefly summarizing the questions and responses is a courtesy to your respondent as well as a check on the accuracy of your notes.

Most editors prefer that you mention major sources within the text of your article. A study of the magazine will tell you whether or not a bibliography should be included at the end of your article.

Research is, indeed, an essential part of being an effective communicator of the Christian faith. And Sherwood Wirt is right: "The professional waits until he has touched all the bases" before sitting down at the typewriter. Developing a personal library, using community resources, reaching out to others, learning time-saving research techniques—these are the bases of research for the aspiring writer.

5

Organize Your Material

For each article we buy, we turn down twenty. Why? Lack of focus, poor Scriptural support, weak anecdotes, sermonic. Some writers just use pen and paper to release deep emotions—that never works.
        —Mike Umlandt, Managing Editor, *Moody Monthly*

Most professionals we know will say the easiest part of writing is putting words on paper. What's difficult is the mental exercise which comes first. For even if you have an article idea in mind, even if you've completed your research, even if you know the piece will be a "how to" or a narrative or a profile, you must still organize the material you have so that it appeals to a reader and is easily understood. And that requires some hard thinking.

Let's begin simply. A well-written article has focus and structure.

Focus

Some writers refer to the focus of an article as its major idea. Others call it the central idea or approach or angle of a piece. Call it what you like. What matters is that your article has it.

To limit and focus their research, seasoned writers work out a tentative major-idea sentence before beginning research for an article. We talked about this in chapter 4. Now is the time to review this sentence.

Has your purpose changed after researching the topic? Did you find a different angle or approach to the subject? What is the major idea you want to get across to the reader *now?*

Don't respond quickly. Read through your notes. Think

about your material. Toss it back and forth in your mind until it begins to take shape and form—until it begins to come together.

When this happens, work on the major idea. Will you keep the original? Revise it? Toss it out? Whatever, write it out as you see it now in one clear, concise sentence. This is the focus for your material. Because it is so important, we write the major idea of an article on a 3 by 5 card and tape it above our desks, referring to it again and again as we write.

Even though you may not always include this sentence in its exact wording in the article, readers should be able to determine your focus after reading the work. Editors often do this. Note some of the focus sentences which editors later added as subtitles to three of the articles we are studying:

Article title: "The Making of a Slowpoke"
Focus: "If I wanted my children to obey certain codes of conduct, I would have to do the same."
Article title: "Reach Out and Write Someone"
Focus: "With a few spare minutes and some warm words, you can touch another life with a letter."
Article title: "The Lights of Hanukkah Shine on Christmas"
Focus: "Few Christians recognize the significance of Hanukkah. Understanding this ancient Jewish celebration can bring added joy to your Christmas."

The entire article should be focused on the major idea. Every part must be directly related to this one point. This will give your article the unity it needs to be effective.

Structure

Like all good writing, the magazine article has a basic organization: beginning, middle, end. This we call structure. The introduction or lead of an article grabs the interest of the reader and gets things going. The conclusion wraps up everything that's gone before in a neat package. We'll discuss both in detail in later chapters.

The middle or body of the article consists of the accumulated information which develops your major idea. It is what you have gleaned from hours of research. Because the process is a selective one, you will seldom use all the information in your file. The material will probably be a mix of facts, statistics, quotations, anecdotes, description, dialogue, and allusions to people, events, or literary works. Until these are organized in some form, you have only a jumble of ideas.

Focusing on the major idea you want to get across to your reader, you must now put this material together in some sort of sequence. English instructors call this sequence an outline or writing plan. Journalists tend to mentally file information as they gather it—sorting it into levels or categories, linking it to information in their memory banks. Making a mental outline while research is in progress has become a habit for them. Until article writing becomes a habit for you, we suggest you give careful attention to the ordering of your notes. Perhaps organizing your notes has never been easy for you. Or perhaps you have never made a writing plan. For this reason, we want to share some tricks of the trade.

If you took your notes on cards or half sheets of paper, these can be shuffled into chronological order, divided into some kind of groups, or arranged in two piles for comparison. When your notes are in order and they all relate to the major idea, you have a writing plan.

Practically all nonfiction writing—from best-selling books to newspaper editorials, from scholarly essays to stories in the smallest magazine—exhibits basic patterns of structure. And these same kinds of organization are repeated again and again.

If you have been studying articles in the magazines you hope to write for, you may have noticed that three basic patterns emerge: illustration, division, and comparison/contrast. Generally one of these is used to organize the article. Then, one or more appear again and again in sections of the article.

Illustration

In this organizational pattern, the writer makes a point, and then explains it by using examples, facts, quotations, analogies, or anecdotes. Or, he may begin with the illustration and build to the point he wants to make.

Sometimes a writer will use one long example to illustrate his point. The narrative article, with a sequence of events arranged in chronological order, does this. Donnie Galloway's article, "Nowhere Else to Go" is a narrative, one long example, which supports his major idea: "God has a purpose for each one of us. He wants us to live, and He'll give us the courage to live, if we just give Him the chance."

"House with a View" by Ellen Watts is another narrative—the story of Mrs. Watts's search for a house overlooking a beautiful mountain. But the story is an illustration with a specific point: as Christians, we should come out of our isolation and look at the view God has put before us. God gave Mrs. Watts a view of half a million people, living within her line of vision, many of whom did not have a personal relationship with Jesus Christ.

In both of these narrative articles, the stories move chronologically to the major idea at the end. Here the point illustrated is sharply drawn.

Often a writer uses this pattern within her article in much shorter units of writing—a paragraph or two. Note the concise examples used to illustrate the point being made in the first sentence of a paragraph from "One Hundred Years of Compassion":

But by far the greatest asset of the Salvation Army is its

soldiers, dedicated Christians whose primary purpose in life is to win others for Jesus Christ. Much of the budget is raised by their own self-denial efforts. Those working in secular full-time jobs are committed to withholding for themselves only what is needed. Their service to the Army programs is voluntary, without pay. The more than 45,000 bandsmen even provide their own uniforms.

In the following paragraphs from "Sorrow's End," Charles Mylander uses both analogy and anecdote:

When a refining company buys a load of silver ore and melts it down, the ore takes a lot of heat before the dross separates from the pure metal. In the life of the Christian the Lord at times puts on the heat until everything impure comes to the top. Then he drains off this dross, leaving greater purity underneath. The refiner's goal is sterling silver; God's goal is proven character.

Elizabeth was a godly pastor's wife fighting a losing battle with cancer. In a quiet and unassuming way she had walked with the Lord for many years. Soon after the discovery of cancer her comments revealed the ongoing purging process. "You would think that after all these years I would not face anything new in my Christian life. But I am learning that the Lord always has something new for us, no matter how long we have been Christians."

The impact of Elizabeth's character was amazing. Her funeral was held in the church where she and her husband Clark last served as pastors. The influence of her life, and her level of maturity in suffering brought friends and acquaintances by the hundreds. God had so purged her character that her final testimony moved many of her friends a step closer to the Lord.

In much the same way, facts, statistics, or quotations are often used to support a point. In "Where the River Jordan

Flows," Jean Barnum illustrated the idea expressed in the first sentence of the paragraph by a series of facts:

> The bright blue Sea of Galilee is in reality not a sea at all, but a fresh water lake. It lies in a deep cup in the hills, around 690 feet below sea level. It's called Lake Kinneret by the people of Israel because it's shaped like a kinnor or harp. The Sea of Galilee is around 13 miles long, and 32 miles around. Its greatest width is eight miles, its greatest depth about 150 feet.

Linda Harris uses quotations in "Are You a Workaholic?" to clarify a definition:

> A speaker at a seminar I attended some time ago defined a workaholic as "a person who must work at everything he or she does." And Marilyn Machlowitz, psychologist and author of *Workaholics,* admits to being a workaholic and says a workaholic "is someone who loves and lives to work."

To use this pattern effectively, you must find the clearest example, the latest facts, the best quotation to illustrate your point.

Division

This organizational pattern occurs when a writer divides the subject of his article into several smaller units in order to explain and simplify it. In "The Child Set in Our Midst," Maxine Hancock uses narrative form but divides her story into three distinct parts: the child, Afshan, had (1) "interrupted us," (2) "interrogated us," and (3) "interpreted anew to us the whole wonderful Christmas event." Each section is developed fully as the author explains the truths which a family can learn from a child.

In his article "To Wake a Meaning," Bruce Hekman uses the division pattern to give us some pointers on promoting the reading of good books. He breaks his suggestions into four sections and discusses each in turn: (1) "Read books aloud!" (2) "Make time for books!" (3) "Make books available!" and (4) "Read books yourself!"

And the division pattern often appears in smaller units. Sometimes the division is by question and answer as in this paragraph from Sherwood Wirt's article, "John Calvin: the Burning Heart":

> What was the essence of Calvinism? The chief characteristic of this "new man?" One might reply by quoting the five doctrinal points in the famed acronym TULIP—total depravity, unconditional election, limited atonement, irresistible grace, and perseverance of the saints. An admirer and disciple of Calvin in the last century, Benjamin B. Warfield of Princeton said, "The Calvinist is the man who has seen God, and . . . is filled on the one hand with a sense of his own unworthiness . . . and on the other hand with adoring wonder that nevertheless this God is a God Who receives sinners."

Other times, the division may be clearly identified by using words like *first, second, third,* or *one, another, and another;* by using a list of reasons; or by using steps in a process. Note the use of the pattern to organize these five paragraphs from Charles Mylander's article, "Sorrow's End":

Four responses

A few people deny the problem exists. A bereaved widow tries to live as if her husband were still present, leaving his clothes and personal belongings undisturbed. Years later everything in the house suggests that he may show up at any minute. But her denial will never bring him back or even help her adjust to a new life. In extreme instances, some people live in an imaginary world and wind up in a psychiatric hospital.

A second response is to try to *grin and bear it.* Accepting the tragedy as some kind of fate, these people trudge through life with a weak smile. In Christian garb, these weary saints moan about "bearing the cross," with little evidence of joy or inner peace. The problem with this attitude is that it acts as if God is on vacation; or if he's indeed out there, he does not care enough to help.

In a strange twist of values, some well-meaning people praise the "grin and bear it" pattern as courage. They fail to discern that their unbelief and attempts at self-sufficiency are stumbling blocks which hinder God from acting in their time of need.

A third reaction, all too common, is to *turn bitter*. Resentment eats away at the human spirit like acid on a battery. In times of suffering, these people blame God or another person involved. The tragedy of bitterness is that it ends up self-defeating.

Wise Christians take the fourth approach, something far more helpful. They determine to *yield to the Lord* to make them better people as a result of the suffering. They do not hide from the shock of the pain, but rather endure it like a patient recuperating from surgery. Yielded Christians can count on him to do at least four things.

In "How to Quarterback Your Own Education," Bruce Dodd, Jr., numbers the three divisions of a paragraph:

The tide of the education game turns dramatically but silently when a student seizes three great thoughts:

1. I am a young person with the primary occupation of student—not just a kid with an obligation to go to school.

2. Success in school will make me happy, since all five measurable elements of happiness in students are related to school achievement.

3. I was born to win—especially in school since learned skills, positive attitudes and hard work are the keys to success.

The dominant characteristic of this method of organizing material is that a topic is divided into parts, and these parts are then discussed in an easily recognized, logical sequence.

Comparison and Contrast

The third major pattern of organization is comparison and contrast. A writer uses this pattern to explain two or more ideas by discussing either their similarities or their differences—sometimes both.

Even the title in Wayne Jacobsen's article, "Gethsemane: A Battle Won . . . A Battle Lost" suggests a comparison. In the article, the responses of Jesus and Peter to the battle of the cross are examined. "The contrast between these two men, now at the Garden and later through the trial," Jacobsen states, "provides an intriguing study on prayer." Jesus is shown as a man who prayed: He prayed honestly; "He settled His commitment to the will of the Father before He prayed"; He looked for His prayer to make a difference." Peter, on the other hand, is shown as a man who slept, who rose to fight the battle in his own strength, who failed by denying the Lord whom he loved. After the results of these two responses are discussed, application is made to our lives.

Look at these three short paragraphs taken from the same article. The comparison and contrast pattern is repeated three times:

> Jesus endured the lies, insults and pain His adversaries heaped on Him without raising voice or hand to free Himself. All Peter could think about by the fire was saving his own neck should they decide to do to Jesus' followers what they were doing to Jesus.
>
> Jesus could already see past His moment of pain. "In the future you will see the Son of Man sitting at the right hand of the Mighty One and coming on the clouds of glory." For the joy set before Him He endured the cross. Peter couldn't see beyond the moment until it was too late and the fruit of his selfishness was bitter weeping.
>
> In the heat of battle, Jesus had proved faithful. He had pre-

pared Himself at the feet of the Father. Peter, forfeiting his opportunity there, endured a night of torture—first with fear and then with failure.

Many times a combination of two or three of these popular organizational patterns is used. For example, study this paragraph from "The Age of Twelve" by Timothy Boyd:

> Every culture sets a time at which they consider their children to move into adult responsibilities. In Jesus' day the Romans, for example, viewed their male children as coming to maturity sometime between the ages of fourteen and seventeen. The exact age was determined by the family, based on a variety of factors. As a new adult the boy was given the right to wear the all-white *toga virilis* (toga of manhood), which marked him as a full citizen of Rome. Greeks, on the other hand, regarded their young men at age eighteen as entering a period of preparation for adult status. At age twenty the Greek male assumed his position as a full citizen. The Jewish male also went through a period of transition from child to adult, but this transition was different from other contemporary cultures in two aspects: (1) The Jewish rites of passage occurred earlier in the life of the boy, and (2) they were dominated by the religious beliefs of Judaism.

Professional writers are not always conscious of using organizational patterns in their writing. Illustrating, dividing material, and comparing things are simply logical ways to organize our thoughts. In Timothy Boyd's paragraph three groups are clearly seen: Romans, Greeks, and Jews. But he is doing more than dividing. He is comparing the time that their male children come to maturity. And he gives examples for each culture. Because he has moved logically from one group to the next, illustrating each in turn, his ideas are clear.

The best way to become comfortable with the process of organizing your material is to study the articles which appear in the magazines for which you hope to write. Look first for the major idea of the article. Then look for the supporting ideas which form the framework. Next, determine what patterns the writer has used to develop these ideas.

Now think about the work you are doing. Are you focused on a major idea? Have you selected the material which will develop it? Do you have a writing plan which includes basic patterns of organization? If your answer is "yes," you are on the right track. You are using your pen and paper to create a carefully-thought-out, well-organized article.

6

Make Contact at the Beginning

The writer's job is to find the argument, the approach, the angle, the wording that will take the reader with him.
—Paul Roberts, Author and Educator

Sentences balanced with rhythm, paragraphs packed with clear, interesting examples, and a conclusion loaded with a powerful impact can all go unread and unpublished unless we make initial contact with the reader.

While this may seem unfair, most of us follow a pattern when we pick up a new issue of a magazine. We skim the table of contents, flip through the pages, return to an article which interests us, and begin to read. Contact! To make that contact effective, the introduction must (1) capture the reader's attention, (2) suggest the major idea of an article, and (3) imply some method of organization to be used.

Capture the Reader's Attention

Why should anyone be interested in what we write? We can't automatically assume that anyone will. Radio, television, conversation, numerous activities—all these compete for reading time. We can't even assume the undivided attention of editors whose desks are stacked high with manuscripts to be read and evaluated.

For these reasons, our lead sentences must capture the reader's attention; they must stop him from turning immediately to another article. We must make contact. But how? Some suggestions:

Use attention-grabbing words, techniques

If the beginning words, the beginning paragraphs, of an article have sufficient impact upon our reader, we may even entice him into a subject which otherwise would not interest him at all. The drama, the humor, the shock we feel about our subject material can be transmitted to our readers through skillful writing techniques.

Examine these introductory devices.

(1) A direct statement of fact:

Christians in our day will either present a clear Christian counter to neopagan values or we will be neutralized and eventually consumed by them.
—Albert L. Truesdale, "Christian Living in a Non-Christian
World"

(2) A question or series of questions:

Want to decrease the conflict and increase the pleasure of your family's daily living? That's what family meetings are doing for us, and they can do the same for you.
—Ann Thompson, "Family Meetings"

(3) An attention-getting initial statement:

On March 26, 1983, my actions suddenly became bizarre. My friends wondered about my mental health; strangers found me exasperating, if not un-American. My odd behavior even earned me scowls and threats, stares and head shaking.

On that fateful day, I began to take speed limits literally.
—Dean Merrill, "The Making of a Slowpoke"

(4) An accumulation of details:

Every dramatic answer to prayer mentioned in the Bible came in a time of trouble. Think of the exodus from Egypt, the crossing of the Red Sea, the wall of Jericho. Recall Gideon with his lamps and trumpets before the Midianites, David with his sling before Goliath, Elijah with his prayer of faith before the prophets of Baal. As one's mind races along the track of Bible history —through kings and prophets of Jesus, John, Peter, and Paul— the same truth stands straight and tall: Every crisis gives God a fresh opportunity to use evil for good.

—Charles Mylander, "Sorrow's End"

(5) An anecdote:

Harold built his business from the ground up. He learned his trade as a teenager. Soon after he was married, he went into business for himself. A new business takes hard work, and Harold was willing to give it. On the outside, he seemed to be a happy, successful, self-confident person. But Harold had some deep problems hidden inside.

Going to church and being a Christian did not seem to bring much joy to Harold. Church and Christianity were more of a duty to him than a privilege.

Harold's oldest son was a disappointment. Though the son was in his early twenties, he often acted like a child. He dropped out of several schools and colleges and could not keep a steady job. Harold's other three children also seemed to be drifting away from the family.

Harold's deepest hurt concerned his business. He had recently built a new building, costing over a quarter of a million dollars. But business began to drop because competitors with less overhead were able to underbid him. Harold put more and more effort into his work but received less and less satisfaction from it.

All of Harold's problems stemmed from one source—his business meant everything to him. His employees, his family, even God and the church were secondary to his work and his success as a businessman. Harold was a workaholic.

—Linda Harris, "Are You a Workaholic?"

(6) An analogy:

Craggy, arthritic sandstone figures jut out of the seemingly endless sea of sand. Windswept dunes change shape like slow-moving clouds. Sand, wind and sun angrily buffet any life persistent enough to reside in the desert. And . . . well, you get the idea. Deserts on the average are dry places and not well liked by the general public. Even our vocabulary is unkind to arid places. We call them *waste* lands or *bad* lands or Death Valley.

Sometimes I open my Bible and hear the hollow, formless wind of the desert eroding my enthusiasm to read Scripture. The voice that reads to me in my head goes monotone, slows down and sometimes whispers, "This is boring." Then I ask myself if reading a Christian comic book would count as having a Quiet Time.

The erosion continues. Not only is Scripture dry, but prayer becomes anhydrous. Soon I am bickering with Christians about stupid things. I am on my way to becoming a craggy, arthritic, sandstone Christian.

Boredom is a hard enemy to fight because we cannot see it. Where does it come from? Must I just wait for it to go away, or can I do something to fight it? As with the water beneath the desert, we need to probe beneath that crusty, lifeless boredom to find the cool, life-giving water of the Word. Here are some things I have learned from my occasional Death Valley Quiet Times.

—Tim Cummings, "Death Valley Quiet Times"

(7) A dialogue or quotation:

Summing up his impressions of the Holy Land's River Jordan, a young tourist said, "Why, compared with the Mississippi, it's hardly more than a stream." Writer Mark Twain once wryly observed: "It's not any wider than Broadway in New York." Even the late David Ben-Gurion, first prime minister of Israel, admitted that his first sight of the Jordan was a great disappointment to him.

—Jean Barnum, "Where the River Jordan Flows"

Often a combination of techniques is used. For example, the brief anecdote which opens the article "100 Years of Compassion" begins with a direct statement of fact containing many details and closes with a quotation.

> On March 10, 1880, George Scott Railton and seven young women, all dressed in Salvation Army uniforms, marched down the gangplank of the steamship *Australia* in New York City and claimed the country for God.
>
> These eight Christians were not the first to stake such a claim in America, but perhaps none were more determined to win souls for Christ and help converts to live victoriously. And, no doubt, the petition of one Christian who bid them farewell in England served to strengthen their determination through the month-long voyage. "Drown 'em on the way, Lord," he prayed, "if they're going to fail You when they get there."

Supply some background information.

Readers of Christian periodicals rightfully expect to understand the articles without doing extensive research. Some subjects require background information, concisely presented. Most people know a little about John Calvin, for example. But look at the amount of information we get from six short paragraphs which begin Sherwood Wirt's article, "John Calvin, The Burning Heart."

> God, the late evangelist Joe Blinco often remarked, has a disturbing habit of laying his hands on the wrong man.
>
> It could be said that God laid His hands on the wrong man in John Calvin. A thin, timid, dyspeptic Frenchman with a scraggly beard, Calvin was basically a scholar who desired nothing better than to spend his life in libraries. Instead, he was thrust into the vortex of Europe's fiercest religious battles. Before he died in 1564 at the age of fifty-four, he had met the challenge, overcome his opposition, and become one of the most influential figures in religious history.

But at a cost. For while his brilliant teaching, writing, and devout spirit had won the respect of millions, his angry polemics, vindictive diatribes, and mistakes of judgment made him one of the most maligned and vilified figures of his century.

Since apostolic times, no one in the history of the Christian church has had as many enemies as Calvin. They insulted him, set dogs on him, fired guns outside his house, and threatened his life. In the halls of government, he was not only attacked for his theology, but on trumped-up charges of immorality. However, Calvin responded in kind; his pen made him an opponent to be feared.

Yet there was a gentleness in Calvin not often mentioned. He knew how to retain the admiration and affection of his friends. During the twenty-seven years he was a pastor in Strasbourg and Geneva, he showed a sensitivity and love for his parish members that is a model for today's ministers. He was tender and affectionate with his wife, Idelette. In her pregnancy, he was solicitous, and heartbroken when their son died. Calvin was a man acquainted with grief. What a strange man he was, but what an impact he made on his generation.

Here's what we now know about John Calvin:

thin	winner	poor judgment
timid	influential religious figure	maligned by many
French	brilliant teacher	had many enemies
scraggly beard	brilliant writer	gentle
scholar	devout spirit	sensitive
fighter	respected by millions	loving
died in 1564	temper	tender, affectionate
died at age 54	vindictive	acquainted with grief

Background information often takes the form of an introduction to someone the reader may not know at all. In the article which Dave Bourne did on Ken Tada, the introduction sets the stage for the interview which follows. Ken Tada is presented as a unique and interesting individual as well as the husband of Joni Eareckson Tada.

Forget for a moment that I was talking to a fellow who's married to one of the best-known Christian women in the country. Or that he's made a life-time commitment to love and care for a wife who's severely disabled.

The fact is, I was talking to a man who's also a very interesting and personable individual: Ken Tada, husband of noted speaker and handicapped activist Joni Eareckson Tada. He teaches social studies and physical education at John Burroughs High School in California and had a free period to talk.

Since their marriage in July 1982, a good deal of material has been published on Joni's views of married life and her ministry. But little has appeared on her husband. This raised a number of questions in my mind.

What's *he* like? How does *he* view married life? How does he define *his* ministry?

Before we go too far, though, let's cover some basics.

The object of my curiosity is a 37-year-old native Californian who spent several years of his childhood in Japan, where his father was an Army major in the U.S. occupation forces there after the Second World War.

A graduate of Cal State University at Northridge (where he earned a B.A. in history), Tada has taught for 14 years at the same high school where he once played football and was student body president.

He's also been involved as a Young Life leader. This seems fitting, as it was through this group's ministry that Tada became a Christian while attending Cal State.

And then there's his wife, Joni.

Background may consist of personal, cultural, historical, biblical information—anything which the reader needs to know. The length of the introduction depends upon the knowledge of the reader and the subject material, but be concise. Move without any unnecessary delay to the major point of the article. *Involve the reader personally.*

Emphasizing the information a reader already knows or has experienced is a good method of beginning an article. Familiar ideas join writer and reader in the introduction to Lin Grensing's article, "The Little Things You May Not Hear":

> The spoken word is a major mode of communication—yet it is by no means the only one. Non-verbal communications also play a vital role in our interaction with others.
>
> The most common types of non-verbal communication are familiar to us all. A nod of the head, a wave of the hand, a frown—each of these conveys a message.

Another approach which can draw the reader into the article is the "you-centered" technique used by Terry Valley to begin his article, "God of the Galaxies, Lord of the Leptons":

> As you read this, you and I are speeding through space at 600,000 miles an hour. That's because Earth is being slung around the center of our galaxy that fast. Yet, even at this fantastic speed, it will take us 200 million years to make one orbit.

All of these introductory writing techniques can stimulate fluency. They get us started. For this reason, too, they are important.

Equally as important to know about are a number of potentially ineffective beginnings—beginnings which no longer stimulate interest because they have been used so frequently or because they fail to meet good writing standards. Would you read articles which began like these?

(1) The dictionary quotation:
     According to *Funk and Wagnalls Standard Dictionary,*

compassion is "pity for the suffering or distress of another with the desire to help or spare." Compassion can be seen in ministers, doctors, teachers, mothers, fathers, and so forth.

(2) The complaint:
After worrying for nearly a week about what God wanted me to write about, I happened to notice a newspaper article about a man who saved his young son from drowning. It was then I decided that others should be thinking about this too.

(3) The truism:
Although there may be times when we think otherwise, honesty is always the best policy.

Another point worth noting here is that all we have said about capturing the reader's attention in the first few lines of your article applies to the title of the work as well. Too often the title is neglected or hastily concocted as a required afterthought.

Ideally, the title of an article alone generates reader interest. At the same time, it suggests the major concern of the paper. Frequently, it expresses the degree of formality and the mood of the article.

Some titles of dubious quality:

"Love"
"Easter Morning"
"Friendship is Golden"
"Reading Your Bible"
"Pastors"

And some which are more effective and made their way into print:

"How to Be Profitably Unemployed"

"Chasing Fleas"
"The World's Most Dangerous Mission Field"
"Candles, Diapers, Soap, and Souls"
"Is Your Focus on Forever?"

Suggest the Focus

The major idea of an article customarily appears at the beginning, as a part of the introduction. Note this example from "The Lights of Hanukkah Shine on Christmas."

> Light from thousands of candles will be seen this month through the windows of both Jewish and Christian homes around the world. For those celebrating Hanukkah, the lights will stand as a reminder of a time in Jewish history when the temple in Jerusalem was restored for worship of God, and the seven lamps of the Menorah once again shone brightly. For those celebrating Christmas, the lights will announce to the world the birth of one who declared, "I am the light of the world."
>
> The Jewish celebration is too often ignored by Christians—perhaps because we know so little about it. Yet, Jesus celebrated the festival and called our attention to it by His teaching. The lights of Hanukkah can have deep significance for those of us who observe the birth of Christ.

Statements about Jewish and Christian homes lighted by candles, and the meaning of Hanukkah and Christmas, lead into the major idea: "The lights of Hanukkah can have deep significance for those of us who observe the birth of Christ." This is the main idea around which the entire article is developed. It is the focal point.

Occasionally, the major idea statement is deliberately withheld until the concluding portion of the paper. When this is done, it is nearly always for reasons of emphasis: a writer feels that his ideas are more impressive if they lead point by point to a conclusion which is the major idea. This type of organization is more difficult to execute successfully than the customary one, but it can be logical and powerful. A good example is Donnie Galloway's article, "Nowhere Else to Go." His main point, the major idea of his article, is in the last two lines: "God has a purpose for each one of us. He wants us to live, and He'll give us the courage to live, if we just give Him the chance."

Indicate the Method of Organization

In addition to capturing the reader's interest and suggesting the focus of an article, the introduction often indicates the organization the writer will follow. This may be simply implied. For example, read Maxine Hancock's introduction to "The Child Set in Our Midst":

> I come from a family of four children. Our Christmases were happy, exuberant affairs. But as we moved into our later teens, Christmas became rather quiet. The old excitement, the irrepressible childish joy in giving, even the over-eating to groan point, all were memories from the past. Murmurs of appreciation for exchanged housecoats and fountain pens replaced whoops of delight over new toys. At the table, polite restraint prevailed. My brother and sisters and I, now into high school and college, were growing up. And something seemed to be missing from Christmas.
> And then came Afshan's Christmas.

We expect the author to tell us how Afshan brought meaning into the celebration of Christmas. And that is exactly what Maxine Hancock does. Later she subtly introduces three words, "interrupted," "interrogated," and "interpreted," and builds the organization and meaning of her article around them.

More often, perhaps, the introduction sets up the organization to come clearly and concisely. Let's take a close look at

Bruce Dodd's introduction to "How to Quarterback Your Own Education":

> Can you imagine a quarterback who practices only when he feels like it, frequently runs to the wrong goal and calls, "Kill the clock!" in the middle of touchdown drives? As ridiculous as it sounds, classroom quarterbacks make these painful mistakes every day. No wonder they fail to see school as great sport.
>
> Students today have more freedom to choose their goals and how to reach them than ever before in the history of American education. A powerful team of both amateurs and professionals respond to the signals they are given.
>
> "What can we do?" concerned parents ask. The media bombards educators for their failures, students and teachers complain about each other and everyone too often suffers in noisy desperation. It's time to call for quiet in the huddle and get the team together.
>
> Unfortunately, there has been a strange conspiracy of silence concerning five critical aspects of the school game plan.

The last sentence of the introduction tells us that the article will be divided into five parts: "five critical aspects of the school game plan." Glancing through the article we find these five sections numbered and introduced with a strong opening statement. In one or two paragraphs the author discusses each statement as a problem and then offers a solution. A critical concern, a movement toward solutions, characterizes the article. The organization suggests the helpful attitude of the author.

Mastering the skills and techniques used by professionals to create effective introductions takes time and effort. With practice, however, you will gain confidence. Soon you will be writing introductions which not only make contact with the reader but take him swiftly into the article and guide him gently through to the end.

7

Reinforce at the End

Many otherwise good writers don't know when or how to stop.
—Hayes B. Jacobs, Author

The conclusion of an article can be the point of greatest emphasis, greatest impact, greatest importance. The reader will remember the last sentences he or she reads—if the words are carefully and clearly written. The writer's objective as he comes to the end of his article is to stamp the major idea indelibly on the reader's mind.

Consider the Length

Naturally the length of a conclusion depends on the writing which precedes it. In a short article which classifies Bible study methods into three types, for example, a one-sentence conclusion following discussion of the third type may be sufficient. If the article involves argument or definition, however, as might be the case if the major idea were "The inner-city church is the testing ground for Christianity," it is wise to bring all the major points of the article together in the conclusion.

In addition, the length of a conclusion should be in proportion to the article itself. Certainly a 600-700 word article does not require more than a short paragraph. Usually a sentence or two is enough. In a longer article, the reader requires more help in recalling the most important ideas presented.

Circle Back to the Major Idea

The major idea of an article generally appears somewhere in the introduction. The body of the article develops the major idea in sections, focusing on one idea at a time. The conclusion brings these parts back together. No new material is introduced; the emphasis in on the focus which the author had in mind from the beginning. For example let's see how Albert L. Truesdale accomplished this in writing his article, "Christian Living in a Non-Christian World."

Introduction

Christians in our day will either present a clear Christian counter to neopagan values or we will be neutralized and eventually consumed by them.

This one-sentence introduction is the major idea of Dr. Truesdale's article.

Body

The first seven paragraphs develop the idea that the "Christian faith was born into a world marked by religious and moral pluralism" but survived. In paragraph eight, Dr. Truesdale states, "our world is experiencing repaganization." He offers six principles to combat this condition.

Conclusion

The six principles are brought together in "our entire mode of conduct." On a positive note we are returned to "a clear Christian counter" demanded in the introduction.

Finally, as Christians, our entire mode of conduct should prepare us to live redemptively among our fellow employees, associates, families, and neighbors. As the Book of James so clearly states, a profession of faith in Christ must legitimate itself in an ethic consistent with what God has said about himself and His world in Christ.

Select an Appropriate Writing Technique

The conclusion must be clearly identified as the last statement. No reader likes to be left wondering if the writer just quit or if the publisher omitted a section. There are myriads of closing techniques, but some are more popular with good writers than others. Try these:

1. *A brief summary:*

> I owe her so much. She taught me the power of love and caring in a way that was new to me. She taught me that the human spirit can endure untold horrors and triumph in the face of terror with consistent, patient caring. She taught me that the love of God, loving through us, can break the strongest barriers and free a spirit to soar.
> —Dick Heinlen and Norma West, "Elizabeth's Return"

2. *A generalization which restates the major idea in different words:*

> Good books touch the heart and nudge the Christian toward the full dimensional obedient life that is our calling.
> —Bruce Hekman, "To Wake a Meaning"

3. *A return to the words or writing devices of the introduction:*
Introduction

My grandmother, who refers to herself as "the tough old bird," can date the change in her character to the year 1906. This was the year of the Great San Francisco Earthquake and the year she began to depend on God. She was 19, a demure and proper young lady, sheltered by her family in the very heart of San Francisco.

Conclusion

Grandmother's straight posture and salt-and-pepper wig express her concern for an orderly appearance. Never does she appear without her pink lipstick and her beaded necklace that coordinate her attire. She greets and dismisses each day with the same determined attitude which she must have adopted when she first saw the ruins of the San Francisco Earthquake and which gained for her the title, "the tough old bird." This toughness stems from the strength she finds in the Lord. "The two of us can do anything," she says with a grin—and she believes it.

—Janet Bollinger, "I Remember the Great San Francisco Earthquake"

4. *A dramatic ending which utilizes some emotion:*

In the terrible, terrible *doing* of ministry the minister is born. And curiously, the best teachers of that nascent minister are sometimes the neediest people, foul to touch, unworthy, ungiving, unlovely, yet haughty in demanding (and then miraculously receiving) love.

Arthur, my father, my father! So seeming empty your death, it was not empty at all. There is no monument above your pauper's grave—but here: it is here in me and in my ministry. However could I make little of this godly wonder, that I love you?

—Walter Wangerin. Jr., "The Making of a Minister"

Another example, less dramatic, in keeping with the tone of the article:

Full and familiar as we try to make them, these little envelopes that follow us from zip code to zip code can't do everything. They can't bring friends to us in person or return us to an old neighborhood we loved. But perhaps they will ease the transition a little, offering handwritten hugs where human arms can't reach.

—Carol C. Crawford, "Reach Out and Write Someone"

A bit of dialogue, a quote from an authority, a strong anecdote, a line from a poem—all these can reinforce the major idea. And that is your objective.

Professional writers avoid at least two types of conclusions:

1. *Plea for understanding:*

> I hope that I have convinced you that only by seeing the mystery of God-become-child can you capture the wonder of Christmas. It is important that you understand this. Please ask yourself how you have responded to the Christ child.

Fortunately, Maxine Hancock wrote a different ending for her article, "The Child Set in Our Midst." No doubt this writer wanted her readers to understand the truth she learned from her experience with the child, Afshan. She knew it would enrich their lives. But she didn't plead with her readers. Note what she did instead:

> Each Christmas, I want to capture again some of the wonder Afshan showed me, some of the awe at the mystery of God-become-Child. I want to stop to really hear the voices of the children in my life—interesting in themselves and pointing to the One who became a child among us. I want to ask myself some questions about how I have responded to the Christ Child. Have I allowed his interruption of my priorities and selfishness? Have I answered his interrogation honestly, crying out from deep within my heart, "You are the Christ . . . and I love you"? Have I worshiped the invisible, immortal God he came to interpret to us, hushed before his holiness?
>
> At this Christmas season, as I gather with other Christians, we will say the family prayer we can say only because of Christmas. I will take a deep breath as I realize again that he who came to us as a child invites me now to come to him as a child. The old words, and the sweet old celebration will be new again as we pray together, "Our Father . . ."

Wouldn't you respond more positively to Mrs. Hancock's technique? She asks herself leading questions, and the reader easily accepts them as his own.

2. *The preachment:*

> You may be one of those Christians who hides in the church along with your prejudices, fighting any change others may suggest. Integrated ministries are God's way, my friend, and you better get your head out of the sand.

Perhaps this is a bit strong, but do you get the idea? The reader is the writer's friend. But it is doubtful if any reader would be willing to have this writer for his friend—or to make any decision for change based on the article.

A far better ending for an article on "breaking new ground" was written by Carol Dettoni for "Changing Their World: An Interview with Tony and Lois Evans." This article is an interview with a couple who saw some needs in the black church and lovingly began to meet those needs. The Evans worked not only to make their church a model for the community, but their family a model for the Christian alternative life-style. With these points in mind, see if you agree that the reader would be far more likely to consider carefully making some changes of his own after reading the article with Carol Dettoni's conclusion.

> Are Tony and Lois Evans really revolutionaries? Perhaps not, but they are clearly breaking new ground in their ministry to the black community. "As far as the ministry is concerned, my pet word is alternative," Tony said. "The church of Jesus Christ is to provide an option for the world. We can't do that if we amalgamate into the world and we can't do that if we run from the world. We must be in the world but not of it. We must be an alternative to it."

What can we learn from all this? Good writers neither plead for their readers to understand nor preach to them. Writers who ignore these cautions reveal a lack of confidence. Are you convinced that what you have said is important? Then let your conclusion reflect strength.

A final suggestion: study the concluding words of newspaper feature writers. Limited space forces them to search for techniques, ways, words, that will leave an impact on the reader.

One idea, one thought—stripped to the bare bone—stamped on the reader's mind: this is your objective for your closing words.

8
Put It All Together

Don't write like a writer—just write.
—Don McKinney, Managing Editor, *McCalls*

By now you're probably up to your eyebrows in the theory, technique, and research involved in writing. You know what you're going to say in your article and how you're going to say it. Some of your information is in your head, but much of it is on notecards. Lay these out before you in the order of your writing plan. Place a dictionary, a thesaurus, pens, and paper within reach. The mental exercise you've gone through pays off now. You know your story. As you follow your writing plan, weaving the notecard information with the thoughts in your head, your article will grow, section by section. So begin.

At this point, whether you write in longhand, on a typewriter or a new word processor, your goal should be to put words on paper as rapidly as you can. Don't be self-conscious about your writing; don't analyze it; above all, don't worry about misspelled words or grammar. Simply tell your story. Double-space your work and leave wide margins on all sides.

McCall's Managing Editor Don McKinney says, "Most stories, if they are any good, will tell themselves. The writer's job is to select what is important, to unify the facts into a sensible structure, and let the facts lead his story forward."

Keep writing. If you can, get everything down before you stop. But if you can't, don't despair. As we write this chapter, we hear plaintive voices: "But nobody gets it right the first time!" and "What do you do when you get bogged down?"

We didn't promise writing would be effortless. But we do believe it's easier when you (1) prepare before you begin and (2) achieve some momentum. To agonize over each sentence is not only slow, but extremely painful.

Certainly you will make false starts. We did when writing this chapter, selecting first one quotation, then another before we were satisfied. When you dislike a sentence, simply X it out and write another. Similarly, you will bog down at times. Then it's time for a cup of coffee, a stretch at the typewriter, a piece of chewing gum. It's amazing how sentences will pop into your head as you put a load of laundry into the washing machine. (Just don't let every break in thought be an excuse for getting away from the hard process of putting those words on paper.)

Many writers go all the way through the first writing of an article before going back for a second look. Others stop and rework at the end of each section of the writing plan. For beginning writers, getting words on paper from the introduction all the way through to the conclusion is better. Seeing several pages of work is encouraging.

The initial writing of an article is called a rough draft with good cause. No writer is completely satisfied with his work at this point. It is still rough, still in the process of "becoming" an article. Now is the time to give it a preliminary reading.

This reading is an overview. You can take care of details later.

Read the Introduction

Will the lead sentence draw the reader into the article? Is the major idea clearly stated? After reading the introduction, will the reader have some idea of the organization the article is to follow? The first paragraph or so of an article sets the tone. If

your subject is a serious one, is there anything about the introduction which would suggest a frivolous attitude? If the article
is to be humorous, is the tone of the introduction light enough?
You may need to change a word, several words, a phrase or
two.

Does your introduction supply enough information? One or
two sentence introductions are fine if your reader has the background for understanding the subject. If not, more details at the
beginning will move her into your story with greater ease. Add
a few sentences if you think they are needed.

Read your introduction aloud. How does it sound? Does it
offer a sense of direction? Suggest a clear understanding of what
to expect? Check to see that each sentence leads to the next and
to the next easily, naturally. Make any necessary changes.

Read the Body

Keep the major idea of the article in your mind as you read.
Do the supporting ideas clearly stand out? Is each of these
related specifically to the major idea?

Once these questions are answered, check for content. Each
supporting idea should be fully developed. You may need to
add a few examples, some facts or figures, quotations, or anecdotes. Only when you are convinced that an idea has been
explained adequately should you continue.

Look at the paragraphs. Do they follow each other in logical
sequence? If not, rearrange them. It's not difficult or time-
consuming if you're using a word processor; it doesn't have to
be with any other method either if you follow the cut-and-tape
technique we've used for years. Simply take scissors and cut in
strips the sentences or paragraphs you wish to rearrange. Then
tape the pieces together in the order you like. If you need to add
material to a paragraph, write it on a separate sheet of paper,
cut the rough draft and splice in the new part. Because you have

double-spaced the rough draft, changing a word or two on the copy is fine, but when you add sentences, cutting and taping keeps the manuscript readable.

What if the paragraphs bump each other, don't flow smoothly? You may need to add some *transitions.* These are words or phrases which refer to preceding ideas and point ahead to what will follow. They are markers which show the reader where you're taking him. Transitions are useful between sentences, between paragraphs, and between sections of an article if the idea does not carry itself.

Transitions may be conjunctions or connecting words such as *and, but, yet, however, therefore, meanwhile,* and *nevertheless.* They may be adverbs like *consequently, finally,* and *similarly.* They may be prepositional phrases like *for instance, for example, in another case,* or numbers such as *first, second, third.* And they may be repetitions or rephrasings of statements already appearing in the article. Let's look at some examples: (The transitional words are in italics.)

Transitions between sentences

> The reasons are too numerous to list here. *But* one very important reason was that the early Christians displayed a set of values that provided a clearcut challenge and option to the pagan moralities.
> —Albert L. Truesdale, "Christian Living in a Non-Christian World"

> His presence once among us means that we must stop to consider who he is and why he came. *And* when we do, our lives are wonderfully interrupted.
> —Maxine Hancock, "The Child Set in Our Midst"

Transitions between paragraphs

> . . . I confess that many times I was so preoccupied with that

loneliness and with the fear of being in the combat zone that I
was not always in touch with the comfort of my faith.

Consequently, the visits to an orphanage run by Roman
Catholic sisters north of Saigon provided moments of sanity
amid chaos.

—Dick Heinlen, Norma West, "Elizabeth's Return"

. . . It is a mistake to leave the reviewing of this latter class
of books to secular magazines that are too often insensitive to
issues that are a part of a Christian's definition of "good" books.

Nevertheless, there are many ways to promote reading of good
books, a habit that needs to be learned early in life and nurtured
by sensitive Christian adults.

—Bruce Hekman, "To Wake a Meaning"

. . . Even if we traveled as fast as anything can travel—186,000
miles per second, the speed of light—it would take us 100,000
years to cross it. That's big. *But* there's more. Science tells us
that there are more collections of billions of stars, called galaxies, out there.

—Terry Valley, "God of the Galaxies, Lord of the Leptons"

Transitions connecting the paragraphs of an article give it
coherence. The longer and more complicated the work, the
greater the need for transitions.

To be clear to a reader, to be of professional quality, your
article must have unity and coherence. It must be built around
one major idea, supported by fully developed points. Sentences
and paragraphs must flow logically from one to the next all the
way through the article.

Read the Conclusion

Does the conclusion have strength, power? Does it wrap up
the article by circling back to the introduction and the major
idea? Be sure that it does not include any new ideas and that

it accomplishes your objective. How do you respond to the concluding words of the article? Do you believe your reader will respond in the same way? If you are not satisfied, now is the time to make some changes.

The first reading of your rough draft may have brought you face-to-face with a few problems. Even writers like novelist William Faulkner have met similar challenges. "There is no mechanical way to get the writing done, no short cut," Faulkner once said. "Teach yourself by your own mistakes; people learn only by error." And he was right.

It is said that Ernest Hemingway rewrote the ending to *Farewell to Arms* thirty-nine times. Not many of us are that persistent. But good writers are not afraid to ask the tough questions about their work and to spend time rewriting. Soon you'll have the answers—the best combination of words that will carry your message through. This is your goal.

9

Smooth Out the Rough

The biggest problem I find in manuscripts is cluttering. Writers simply do not provide a clear word picture sufficient for the average reader today.

            —Jack Gulledge, Editor, *Mature Living*

Fatigue, relief, joy—you may be feeling all three as you contemplate those tattered, taped-together pages in front of you. Hours of prayer and hard work have gone into your rough draft; only the final typing remains.

But wait. Don't change the typewriter ribbon yet. If you're like most of us, your article is still rough in spots. You owe it to yourself to polish your manuscript until it glows.

To begin this final task, we suggest that first you do nothing. Yes, nothing. Drop your article into a drawer and forget it. Leave it while you go on to something else: housecleaning, yard work, church activities, or rest and recreation.

Why? Because when you pull it out again in two or three days you will be able to give the article a fresh look. You will have gained some of the objectivity a first-time reader has. Surprisingly, things you've never seen before will jump out at you: a misspelled word, an unclear sentence, a meaningless phrase.

A final, critical reading allows you to examine your language for accuracy, clarity, and strength, and your sentences for conciseness, rhythm and variety.

Choosing the Right Language

Accuracy

As a Christian writer, it is especially important that you verify the truth of what you write. Another phone call or reference check is worth the time it takes to be certain of a date, a street address, or a quotation. Similarly, seeking permission for a quotation is preferable to worrying about its length under copyright laws. Your honesty is judged by the accuracy of your facts.

Accuracy applies to language as well as content. Check grammar and usage. Do nouns and verbs agree in number? A "they says" or a "he were" can mar your story. Are you using the correct word? All too frequently some words are confused: *effect* for *affect,* for example, or *there* for *their* or *it's* for *its.* Be certain. Check a grammar handbook.

Clarity

E. B. White once said, "The main thing I try to do is write as clearly as I can." This, he explained, was because he had the greatest respect for his reader. We agree with Mr. White that good writing should be clear and easy for the reader to understand.

Your choice of words contributes to clarity. The more specific a word, the more clear; the more general, the greater risk of its being fuzzy. The word *church,* for example, is abstract (general) because it can refer to the body of Christ, to a denomination, or to a building. The word becomes more specific when we write "Christ's *church* on earth," "The United Methodist *Church,*" or "the Baptist *church* at 1517 Elm Street." Another example: The word *missionary* is more abstract than *medical missionary.* Both terms are more abstract than "John Smith, Southern Baptist *medical missionary.*" Words like *trust, love, sin, regeneration, salvation* are part of the Christian vocabulary, but they are general and carry slightly different meanings from denomination to denomination. Consider your readers and be aware of these differences. You may need to clarify some meanings.

Words have another dimension as well. They have *denotative* and *connotative* meanings. Denotation is the dictionary or literal meaning of a word while connotation is the personal or emotional meaning of a word. Denotative meanings are essentially stable while connotative meanings differ from person to person because of the experiences we associate with a word. The words *born again, Christian,* and *saved* are good examples of words which carry both denotative and connotative meanings. Think through the words you are using to be sure their meanings are clear.

Sometimes words are figurative in nature. This means that they are used in nonliteral or symbolic ways. The Psalms of the Bible offer outstanding examples of figurative language as do many other books of the Bible. God is referred to as a "rock," "shield," "shepherd," and "word" (89:26; 3:3; 23:1; 119:49). He is personified as writers speak of "the Father," the "right hand of God," and "his feet like unto fine brass" (John 6:45; Rom. 8:34; Rev. 1:15).

Tim Cummings in his article, "Death Valley Quiet Times," speaks of Bible study as a "mental feast," of learning spiritual truths as sitting "at the feet of our Lord," and of "murdering the text." The focus of his article is based on figurative language as he compares devotions without awareness of God's presence to a dry desert with no streams of water.

Bruce Dodd, Jr., does something similar in his article: "How to Quarterback Your Own Education." He uses the game of football as a metaphor for the academic game played with students' education. By using the language of football ("team," "benched," "coach," "skills of the game," "touchdown"), he carries the metaphor from the title to the concluding remarks.

Strength

Words can either be weak or strong. Let's apply this statement to more uses of figurative language. The expressions "old as the hills" and "fresh as a daisy" have been overused and no longer have any power. But consider Sherwood Wirt's identification of John Calvin as the man with the "burning heart" and Bruce Hekman's comparison of good books to "tent pegs" which anchor us in the truth. These are new—and strong. Avoid timeworn clichés; fresh ideas have strength.

Examine your verbs. Writing gains vigor when we select strong, active verbs as Tim Cummings does in "Death Valley Quiet Times." The desert "erodes" his enthusiasm for Bible study. He "bickers" with Christians and "leashes" his imagination. In telling his experience in "Nowhere Else to Go," Donnie Galloway says that he "swerved," "groped," "kicked," "gasped," "choked," "hollered," and "fought."

Both Cummings' and Galloway's verbs are in the *active voice* and almost jump from the page. In contrast, verbs in the *passive voice* frequently seem lifeless, as in "The music *was provided* by the Central City Bell Choir," versus "Central City's Bell Choir *rang* out their songs of praise." In active voice, the subject of a sentence performs the action. In passive voice, the subject is acted upon and the object becomes subject. In lively, informal writing, the active voice predominates. Reserve the passive for instances in which nothing else works.

Selecting the Best Arrangement

Conciseness

In concise writing, every word is essential. Not one word can be deleted without altering an intended meaning. The writing is spare, not spontaneous. To achieve conciseness, ruthlessly cull your manuscript of "say nothing" words or constructions like *sort of* or *kind of* or *seems to be.* Don't use several words if one will do. For instance, *at this point in time* can be reduced to *now. In this day and age* can be reduced to *today.* Something *of great importance* is probably *important.*

Try substituting short grammatical constructions for longer ones. Use phrases for clauses or adjectives for phrases.

Study this lengthy version:

When bedtime came, we found that we had a growing list of "possibles," twin headaches from having squinted so long, and increasingly negative thoughts.

And the original:

Bedtime found us with a growing list of "possibles," twin head-aches from having squinted so long, and increasingly negative thoughts.
—Ellen Watts, "House with a View"

A concise sentence is not necessarily a short one. In the following example, conciseness was achieved by combining several sentences.

First, the lengthy version:

After he had had this encounter, Jesus returned home. He was with Mary and Joseph. He knew that he must mature and prepare for his ministry.

The original:

After this encounter, Jesus returned home with Joseph and Mary to continue maturing and preparing for his ministry.
—Timothy N. Boyd, "The Age of Twelve"

Overused adjectives such as "beautiful," "usual," and "fantastic," and adverbs such as "very," "extremely," and "exceptionally," clutter a sentence. The rule for good article writing is the fewer adjectives and adverbs the better.

Rhythm

Rhythm is the movement of words as we read a work aloud, or feel that we hear as we read silently. For sentences have a definite movement: from the awkward jerks of the beginning writer to the melodic rhythm of the gifted artist. Some writers are particularly skilled at creating rhythm in their work. In addition to increasing the reader's pleasure, rhythm suggests the relationship of ideas and emphasizes the important ones, for units of sound may also be units of meaning. The examples below have been typeset in a form to illustrate this point.

Carol Dettoni, in "Changing Their World: An Interview with Tony and Lois Evans," uses repetition for rhythm and emphasis in a pair of sentences:

> When Dad went to witness,
>   I would be there.
> When he was on the corner handing out tracts,
>   I would be there.

Notice that the author repeats grammatical constructions as well as words. Her repetitions are dramatic. In addition, they emphasize key ideas.

Note the rhythm created by the parallel structures in this sentence from "100 Years of Compassion":

> Those of us in America know well
>   their "doughnut girl" of World War I,
>   their familiar uniforms operating USO's for
>   servicemen in World War II,
>   their coffee and doughnut stations in disaster areas,
>   emergency relief wagons,

Christmas kettles
and brass bands.

Repetition of the word "their" also emphasizes the unique activities of the Salvation Army.

Because sentence rhythm is largely determined by the *effect* we want our sentences to have upon a reader, even so small a rhythmic element as a conjunction can be significant. The following groups of words from the article "Reach Out and Write Someone" actually form one sentence, separated by periods yet held together by conjunctions. The rhythm is slow and the reader anticipates the additions with each "and":

> So I hang on to the note from my mother telling me not to join the Air Force without asking her first. And the letter my sister wrote advising me to get a dog to help fill up my lonely apartment. And the card from a California friend saying of course I should take the new job.

Short sentences through a work can establish a brisk, no-nonsense mood, while longer sentences may convey a thoughtful or contemplative attitude. Generally, the more formal the writing, the more elaborate the sentence structure; the more informal the writing, the greater the liberties a writer may take with traditional forms.

Variety

To avoid monotony, professional writers use a variety of sentence structures. If you want your writing to be interesting, not sing-song, follow their example.

Try using sentences of different lengths. Note the variety in structure and length of sentences in this paragraph from Wayne Jacobsen's article, "Gethsemane, A Battle Won . . . A Battle Lost":

> Finally, Jesus looked for His prayer to make a difference. It was

not a ritual. He was distressed. If it took three times before the throne to deal with it, then three times he would go.

In the same article, Jacobsen uses questions followed by answers to give variety. For example:

How often do we stop praying before our anxieties, fears or doubts are really dealt with? That wasn't an option for Jesus.

Try different structures to begin sentences:

Even if we have disagreements, the thing that brings us closer together is that we're committed to one another.
　　　　　—Dave Bourne, "Ken Tada: Lessons in Love"

There were newspapers strewn all over the floor.
　　　　　—Walter Wangerin, Jr., "The Making of a Minister"

Not only were we making all the rules for behavior, we were also planning all the pleasant things, such as birthday parties and outings.
　　　　　—Ann Thompson, "Family Meetings"

Into this kaleidoscope came the Christians, initially viewed by many as just more clutter on the confusing first-century religious landscape.
　　　　　—Albert L. Truesdale, "Christian Living in a Non-Christian
　　　　　World"

That's big. But there's more.
　　　　　—Terry Valley, "God of the Galaxies, Lord of the Leptons"

As you strive to make your language more accurate and clear, as you arrange words for conciseness, rhythm, and variety, you are developing a personal writing style. And this takes time. With each piece of writing you will become more aware of the techniques which can make your work more interesting and vital. Eventually, you will become comfortable with your writing style—and confident in your judgment of good writing.

But at this point, your manuscript is even more tattered than before. You have read it, marked it, rearranged it, and approved its passage through the final checklist.

Now you can change that typewriter ribbon, for the next step is the last. Soon your manuscript will be ready to mail.

10
Submit

I love being a writer. What I can't stand is the paperwork.
                                        —Peter de Vries, author

Once a manuscript has been corrected and revised, the beginning writer often looks for the quickest way to get it into final form and into the mail. Big mistake. We may agree with Peter de Vries that creating an article is more fun than adding the final touches, but editors are adamant about neatness. Brian Dill, former editor at David C. Cook Publishers, once commented, "I almost prefer subpar copy that is neat to brilliant copy that is not neat."

If you want your article to be read by an editor, don't join the ranks of those who send in sloppy manuscripts with words crossed out, three or four staples in the corner, and scribbled handwritten notes attached for cover letters. Unfortunately, editors receive many of these. Instead, submit a well-prepared manuscript package; it will stand out in any editorial office.

Here are the standards which will give your article a head start once it reaches the publisher:

1. Use 8 1/2 by 11-inch white paper, 16 to 20-pound weight. Erasable bond irritates most editors as it reflects light, making the print difficult to read. More than this, it smudges.

2. Be sure your typewriter ribbon is dark black, and that all typewriter keys are clean. (Of course the manuscript must be typed. We know of no publisher who accepts handwritten copy.)

3. Use one side of the paper only.

4. Set margins for 1 1/2 inches on all four sides and double-space the entire manuscript.

5. Type your name, address, and phone number in the upper left corner of page one, the rights being offered and approximate number of pages in the upper right corner. Most magazine articles are "First Rights," meaning that the article has not been published before. If it has, write "Second Rights" and explain in your cover letter when and where it was first published.

6. Center the title of your article (all capital letters) about 1/3 of the page down and your name two spaces below the title. Skip three or four spaces and begin your first paragraph.

7. Type your last name in the upper left corner of all succeeding pages and the number of each page in the upper right corner.

8. Use a paper clip to hold pages together. Never staple.

9. Write a brief cover letter and enclose a SASE (self-addressed, stamped envelope).

10. Enclose the manuscript in a 9 by 11 1/2-inch manila envelope if you have more than five pages. Fewer than five pages may be folded once and placed in a 6 by 9 manila envelope.

Before you seal the envelope, be sure there are no typing errors, smudges, or coffee stains on the manuscript. These are sure signs of carelessness and will not gain you points with editors.

11. If you have photographs to send, enclose them in the same package. Most magazines pay extra for 35mm color slides or 8 by 10 black-and-white, glossy prints which illustrate articles. Slides should be numbered and placed in a plastic insert sheet, with an identification page attached. A sturdy cardboard

backing in the package will protect photographs from shipping damage.

12. Use first-class mail. The manuscript will arrive in less time and in better condition. Be sure to stamp the outside of the envelope "First Class."

You now have all the tools of the trade that you need to become a "published writer." But Paul's advice to Timothy was to "study" (2 Tim. 2:15), and we suspect he meant that as a continuing process. Floyd Thatcher in the Foreword of *Religious Writers Marketplace* said, "Any writer—especially one involved in communicating religious ideas and feelings—must earn the right to be read." We agree. The Christian writer's goal is excellence. God's work demands our very best.

When, in time, your work expresses God's love, helps those who are struggling with problems, instructs those who are growing, and comforts those who grieve, you will have the joy that comes from speaking "to the hearts of people about Jesus."

Articles

Barnum, Jean. "Where the River Jordan Flows." *Sunday Digest,* 4 Oct. 1981, pp. 2-3+.

Bourne, Dave. "Ken Tada: Lessons in Love." *Christian Life,* May 1984, pp. 20-24.

Bollinger, Janet. "I Remember the Great San Francisco Earthquake." *Mature Living,* Jan. 1983, pp. 12-13.

Boyd, Timothy N. "The Age of Twelve." *Biblical Illustrator.* Spring 1984, pp. 82-84.

Crawford, Carol C. "Reach Out and Write Someone." *Today's Christian Woman,* Fall 1983, pp. 74-75.

Cummings, Tim. "Death Valley Quiet Times." *His,* Mar. 1983, pp. 22-25.

Dettoni, Carol M. "Changing Their World: An Interview with Tony and Lois Evans," *Family Life Today,* Jan. 1983, pp. 12-15.

Dodd, Bruce C., Jr. "How to Quarterback Your Own Education." *Family Life Today,* Oct. 1983, pp. 6-8.

Galloway, Donnie. "Nowhere Else to Go." *Guideposts,* Jan. 1984, pp. 18-19.

Grensing, Lin. "The Little Things You May Not Hear." *Seek,* 18 Mar. 1984, pp. 2-3+.

Hancock, Maxine. "The Child Set in Our Midst." *Christian Herald,* Dec. 1981, pp. 40-44.

Harris, Linda. "Are You a Workaholic?" *Home Life,* Sept. 1983, pp. 18-20.

Heinlen, Dick, as told to Norma West. "Elizabeth's Return." *The Lutheran,* 7 Mar. 1984, pp. 8-9.

Hekman, Bruce. "To Wake a Meaning." *Presbyterian Journal,* 7 Dec. 1982, pp. 6-7.

Jacobsen, Wayne. "Gethsemane: A Battle Won . . . A Battle Lost," *Charisma,* Apr. 1984, pp. 46-47.

Merrill, Dean. "The Making of a Slowpoke." *Moody,* Apr. 1984, pp. 111-112.

Mylander, Charles. "Sorrow's End." *Eternity,* Mar. 1984, pp. 27-28+.

Ricks, Chip. "100 Years of Compassion." *Worldwide Challenge,* Jan. 1981, pp. 33-35.

_____. "The Lights of Hanukkah Shine on Christmas." *Worldwide Challenge,* Dec. 1981, pp. 5-6.

Thompson, Ann. "Family Meetings." *Living with Children,* Jan. Feb. Mar. 1984, pp. 22-23.

Truesdale, Albert L. "Christian Living in a Non-Christian World." *Herald of Holiness,* 29 Jan. 1984, pp. 10-11.

Valley, Terry. "God of the Galaxies, Lord of the Leptons." *Light and Life,* Feb. 1984, pp. 12-13.

Wangerin, Walter, Jr. "The Making of a Minister." *Christianity Today,* 17 Sep. 1982, pp. 16-18.

Watts, C. Ellen. "House With a View." *Live,* 13 May 1984, pp. 2-3.

Wirt, Sherwood. "John Calvin: The Burning Heart," *Moody,* Nov. 1977, pp. 118-121.

Where the River Jordan Flows
by Jean Barnum

Summing up his impressions of the Holy Land's River Jordan, a young tourist said, "Why, compared with the Mississippi, it's hardly more than a stream." Writer Mark Twain once wryly observed: "It's not any wider than Broadway in New York." Even the late David Ben-Gurion, first prime minister of Israel, admitted that his first sight of the Jordan was a great disappointment to him.

Little wonder that the traveler is dismayed when he or she gazes at the historic river for the first time—the Jordan is no more than 15 feet deep, 100 feet wide, and less than 200 miles long. In the summer, when the river is low, there are certain places where a child can safely wade across its shallow waters.

And yet, despite its unimpressive size, dozens of hymns, spirituals, and folk songs have been written about the Jordan, as well as countless pages of prose and poetry. And appropriately so—glorious history was made along its banks. In fact, no other river is referred to as often in the Bible.

It was across this river that Joshua led the Israelites into the Promised Land. On these shores John the Baptist preached—

Reprinted from *Sunday Digest,* © 1981 David C. Cook Publishing Co, Elgin, IL 60120. Used by permission.

clothed in a rough camel's hair garment with a leather girdle strapped about his loins. In these waters lepers were cured.

The traditional site of the baptism of Jesus is a quiet stretch of the river five miles from the Dead Sea. It's a tranquil spot where willows, tamarisks, and flowering bamboo grow along the steep banks—and sparrows chirp among blossoms and reeds.

This is the hallowed place where, for centuries, pilgrims traveled thousands of miles from Russia to commemorate Christ's baptism. At dusk, as many as 60,000 pilgrims at a time, wearing white cotton shrouds and carrying lighted candles, waded into the gently swirling current to immerse themselves in the holy waters. Later, the shrouds were hung on reeds to dry and carefully packed for the long journey home. They were kept until the day the pilgrim died, then served as his burial garment.

The birthplace of the Jordan River is on the slopes of Mount Hermon, over 9,100 feet tall, in southern Syria. A Jewish legend tells us that when God gave Moses the Ten Commandments on Mount Sinai, all the other mountains in the Holy Land muttered that God was showing favoritism. Why Sinai? One little hill called Hermon burst into tears. To console it, God decreed that henceforth it would be the noblest mountain in the land and would wear a crown of snow. The teardrops Hermon shed became one of the sources of the Jordan.

The valley through which the Jordan flows is part of the deepest crack in the earth's crust, a colossal ditch that starts at Hermon's foot and runs over 4,000 miles into eastern Africa.

Leaving Mount Hermon, the Jordan River winds through the green and fertile Huleh Valley, tumbles down to mingle with the waters of the Sea of Galilee, then loops and twists its way through the Valley of the Jordan, and comes at last to rest in the infamous Dead Sea, often called "the graveyard of all water."

Many centuries ago, volcanic eruptions spewed lava across the path of the upper Jordan, blocking the river so that it overflowed its banks and formed a vast swampland and a lake called Huleh.

The marsh was a paradise of nature, alive and vibrant with fish, exotic birds, water buffalo, and wild boar. Here, too, in the still and shallow waters of the swamp, grew great jungles of papyrus. The excellence of the Huleh papyrus was renowned. The ancient Egyptians used it as writing paper.

Now the swamp has been drained by the Israeli government because millions of gallons of much-needed water was being wasted in the marshland. Seven hundred and fifty acres of the old Huleh region have been preserved as a nature and wildlife sanctuary. Much of the papyrus was lost, but the nature reserve still contains some of the best papyrus to be found.

The barrier of ancient lava was blasted away to free the course of the river. Today the Jordan meanders through 15,000 lush acres of flower gardens, rice fields, and sugar plantations. Peanuts and cotton also now flourish in this scenic valley.

South of Huleh, the Jordan drops steeply for the next ten miles on its way to the Sea of Galilee, tumbling wildly down a narrow staircase of rocks and boulders in a continuous series of singing waterfalls. Along the slopes grow thick clumps of oleander and wild *Ziziphus,* the Christ's-thorn, a spiky bush from which the crown of thorns may have been made. Its delicious fruit is prized by shepherds and wild jackals alike.

As the Jordan approaches the Sea of Galilee, the river is more than a thousand feet lower than it was at birth. In Hebrew, the Jordan is called Yarden, "the river that goes down" or "The Descender."

The bright blue Sea of Galilee is in reality not a sea at all, but a fresh water lake. It lies in a deep cup in the hills, around 690 feet below sea level. It's called Lake Kinneret by the people of Israel because it's shaped like a kinnor or harp. The Sea of Galilee is around 13 miles long, and 32 miles around. Its greatest width is eight miles, its greatest depth about 150 feet.

There's an old Hebrew saying, "God created the seven seas, but the Sea of Galilee was His delight." Gulls and herons dip for fish in the shimmering gem-like waters. The warm, mild climate can be compared to that of Florida. In early spring the surrounding hills are awash with almond blossoms, bright scarlet poppies, wild tulips.

But sudden and unexpected squalls frequently sweep down across the lake, whipping ripples into fierce waves. It isn't difficult then to imagine the anxiety of the disciples, huddled together in a pitching boat, while Jesus, arms outstretched, rebuked the wind and calmed the angry sea.

Cafes and hostelries along the waterfront specialize in seafood. One favorite with the travelers is St. Peter's fish, a type very likely caught in these waters by Simon Peter himself.

Today it's customary to see the unruffled lake dotted with white sails, brightly painted fishing boats, and launches speeding by with water-skiers in tow. Young people in swimsuits pedal water cycles across the water, laughing and shouting to one another. But the low hills and the blue waters of Galilee, the wild flowers and the locust trees, and the pink hush of morning are the same as when Jesus and His friends walked along these shores.

The Jordan streams into the northern end of the lake, mingles with Galilee's waters and reemerges at the southern end of the lake to continue its downhill journey to the Dead Sea. It winds over 150 miles through farmland, tangled wilderness, and scorching desert until it empties into the Dead Sea, lowest inhabited spot on earth, 1,300 feet below sea level.

In the Old Testament, the Dead Sea is most often called the Salt Sea. But it goes by many other names. Arabs have called it the Stinking Sea, or the Sea of Overwhelming. An eminent archaeologist, Nelson Glueck, described it in unflattering terms as "the witches' brew now known as the Dead Sea." Others have called it the Bitter Sea and the Prisoned Sea.

This is the death place for the holy river. The Jordan and other smaller streams daily pour an average of several million tons of fresh water into the Dead Sea, but here the journey ends. The Dead Sea has no outlet.

With much water lost by evaporation and with no way for the minerals to be drained out, the Dead Sea has become extremely salty, with nine times more salt content than that of our oceans. Fish that are swept in by the Jordan die in a matter of minutes. No sea life can survive in these waters.

But excellent bathing facilities, as well as overnight accommodations, are offered at a seaside hotel, and swimmers enjoy floating like corks in the buoyant salty water. It's impossible to sink.

The Dead Sea often lies shrouded in a gauze-like mist caused by the intense heat. The water is almost white near the shoreline, gradually changing to emerald, then to deep blue. Barren limestone cliffs rise above the sea to the east. Rock salt, lava, and sulfur streak its beaches.

In the hazy distance in the mountains overlooking the Dead Sea are the crumbled ruins of Machaerus, the great palace where Salome danced before Herod and won the severed head of John the Baptist.

In the lonely cliff region at the northwestern end of the sea, a Bedouin shepherd boy searching for a lost goat wandered into a dark cave and found the earthenware jars that contained the greatest archaeological find of this century—the Dead Sea Scrolls.

Perhaps, compared with the larger rivers of the world, the Jordan does seem small and unimportant. But to those who love her, it's not the size of the Jordan that matters so much. Rather, it's the great and glorious events this river has seen.

Ken Tada: Lessons in Love
by Dave Bourne

Forget for a moment that I was talking to a fellow who's married to one of the best-known Christian women in the country. Or that he's made a lifetime commitment to love and care for a wife who's severely disabled.

The fact is, I was talking to a man who's also a very interesting and personable individual: Ken Tada, husband of noted speaker and handicapped activist Joni Eareckson Tada. He teaches social studies and physical education at John Burroughs High School in California and had a free period to talk.

Since their marriage in July 1982, a good deal of material has been published on Joni's views of married life and her ministry. But little has appeared on her husband. This raised a number of questions in my mind.

What's *he* like? How does *he* view married life? How does he define *his* ministry?

Before we go too far, though, let's cover some basics.

The object of my curiosity is a 37-year-old native Californian who spent several years of his childhood in Japan, where his father was an Army major in the U.S. occupation forces there after the Second World War.

A graduate of Cal State University at Northridge (where he earned a B.A. in history), Tada has taught for 14 years at the same high school where he once played football and was student body president.

He's also been involved as a Young Life leader. This seems fitting, as it was through this group's ministry that Tada became a Christian while attending Cal State.

And then there's his wife, Joni.

Q Just for the record, Ken, when and where did you and Joni first meet?

A The first time I saw Joni she was the featured speaker at a Young Life Banquet. This was in 1980 or '81. Actually I didn't really know who she was at the time, and I didn't get a chance to talk to her that night. But I *was* very impressed by what she had to say.

A year later, we both were attending Grace Community Church, our church home, and this time, she saw me.

Q Did she work up the courage to talk to you?

A Well, the story she tells is that she prayed for the back of my head.

Q Excuse me?

A She was seated behind me in church, and John MacArthur, who's the pastor there, wasn't preaching that day. So since the sermon wasn't real exciting, Joni says her attention wandered and she more or less picked out the back of my head and just started praying for me.

She caught a glimpse of me as I was leaving the church, but we still didn't actually meet until later on, when we were introduced through some friends. Then she recognized me as the person she had prayed for.

Q Ken, despite its many blessings, marriage is a fairly formidable commitment for any couple to make. Did Joni's handicap, and the considerable amount of care you knew she'd require, cause you to have any second thoughts about whether you were really equipped to marry a disabled person?

A No, mainly because we had dated for quite a while, and I had a pretty good idea as to what it was going to take. We had discussed a lot of things. One of the great parts of our dating life, in fact, was that we were very open with each other about her handicap.

When we started talking about marriage, though, some folks thought that maybe it would be a good idea for us to spend some time living with each other. They sort of took the attitude that if we could live together first, and if it worked out, we could go ahead and get married. But because of our Christian beliefs, and the fact that this would really dishonor God, it wasn't even a consideration for us.

But to get back to your question, I think anybody who's married, whether it be to a person who's disabled or not, goes through certain periods of adjustment. You may just have different adjustments to make when you marry someone who's disabled.

Q So you had no hesitation about getting married?

A Well, in a lot of ways, I think marriage is like becoming a Christian. You get to a certain point, and then you have to take that step of faith. If you hold back, you're never going to find what's out there. When it comes down to it, you'll never really know until you make that final commitment.

Q Is there a key to marriage, as you see it?

A I'm a firm believer that the key in any marriage focuses around commitment. With commitment, after all the bubbly feelings of love, the excitement, the early effervescent feeling you get from being in love—after all that settles down, you still have *love*. I don't mean that after getting married you lose those feelings. But when two people in love really focus their priorities around Jesus Christ, there's more to marriage than that first initial reaction.

Even if we have disagreements, the thing that brings us closer together is that we're committed to one another. I think a favorite portion of Scripture for us is James 1, when he talks about trials. If you can think of it in a positive way, even with disagreements and trials, we can grow closer.

Q Have your thoughts about the Church affected your role as a husband?

A Oh yeah. I've been particularly influenced by the book of Ephesians. I think I've also been influenced by two men for whom I have a great deal of respect: John MacArthur and James Dobson. Their thoughts on marriage have been really helpful. In fact, John was the person who married us.

Q How would you define your role as a husband in light of what you've been studying in Ephesians?

A Well, Ephesians talks about how, as husbands, we are to love our wives as Christ loved the Church. And the fact that Christ died for the Church means He made quite a sacrifice—the ultimate sacrifice.

I feel my role as a husband is to look after Joni, not just because she's disabled, but because she's my wife. I really must seek out the best for her in terms of her spiritual needs. I just can't play the role of "head" of our household.

And I know, continuing on in Ephesians, that Joni feels she needs to be subservient to me. Not so much in terms of being a slave or a secondary person—on the contrary, I seek out her advice. But when the final decisions need to be made, I make them. Of course, there's mutuality involved. It's really like teamwork—and we're on the same ball club. We're not working *against* each other, but *with* each other.

Q What are some of the other learning experiences you and Joni are undergoing?

A I think we've experienced some unique situations in our marriage. For example, if we disagree, we believe—as Ephesians tells us—that the sun must not go down on our anger. Now that might mean we have to stay up long hours to resolve a situation. I mean, if Joni wants to go to sleep, she just can't go to bed, pull the covers over her head and not talk to me—because *I'm* the one who's putting her to bed.

So it's almost impossible for us *not* to talk things out before we go to sleep. It's tough to do that sometimes, because we have to confront things a lot quicker. But that's just one example of how a disability can work to our advantage.

We've also had the opportunity in this last year and a half to just learn and see how the Joni and Friends and People Plus ministries have touched so many people's lives. That's exciting.

Q What's your role in Joni and Friends?

A Well, first of all, I'm on the Board of Directors. Secondly, I've been involved in some speaking and teaching in our People Plus program. And, at times, when I've gone with Joni to her seminars, I'll speak to folks there.

Q What are the specific purposes of Joni and Friends and People Plus?

A Joni and Friends has a real burden that the churches of the United States—and the world—get involved in special ministries programs to the disabled. Ten percent of the population in the United States today is made up of disabled folks. But only five percent of the churches make accommodations for them or have special ministries programs. So our function with the seminars is to alert churches to what they could do in this area, and how they can open up doors for special ministries. That's kind of a wide function.

Now the People Plus program is an offshoot of the seminars.

It's a more specific, hands-on approach to what you can do to help someone who's disabled. It teaches folks about different types of disabilities, about attendant care, how to push wheelchairs, how to care for someone who is handicapped. The response to these seminars has been good, too.

Q In light of your work with Joni and Friends, do you see yourself continuing your teaching career or do you think you might eventually work with this ministry full time?

A Well, I've been open to change. But for a long time my prayer has been that I would not get out of teaching unless God was directing me to another area. Now Joni and Friends is certainly an important ministry. But at this particular time, there really isn't a position that I would feel free to get into.

There has been some talk, though, of perhaps starting an independent living center here in Southern California. Now in that sense, I would be able to fit in. But at the present, the role I have in Joni and Friends is as Joni's husband. What happens later on down the line, I'll just have to wait and see.

Q Being married to a disabled person, do you increasingly find yourself seeing life through the eyes of someone who's handicapped?

A Yes, I do. You know, I've often thought about that, but no one has ever asked me about it before. Yeah, I'll go to an airport, and the first thing I'll do is look for an elevator—even when Joni's not there!

It's becoming almost like a second nature. I'll go into a facility and count how many steps there are. I'll look for curb cuts. And if I go into a parking lot and see someone parked in a spot for the handicapped who obviously isn't handicapped, I'll get a little more upset then I would have before I knew Joni. It's just because I know those spots are there for a reason. And some of these folks are taking advantage of them.

But it's true, through second nature, I just look for the obvious things now. Like how to go up and down curbs by yourself in a powered wheelchair. I've just picked these things up from being with Joni. My mind just automatically scans and evaluates situations much faster now.

Q Ken, you're married to someone who has, shall we say, a very high visibility in the Christian community. I don't want to be blunt about it, but do you ever feel people put you in Joni's shadow? Are you ever introduced as Mr. Eareckson?

A Well, because I'm oriental, it's a little hard to mistake me for an Eareckson.

No, that's an honest question and let me answer it this way. I think that perhaps if our's were a secular marriage, there might be a problem. A lot of times when we go out, people don't mean to be rude, but they'll focus on Joni because of that high visibility thing. But she'll make a point of saying, "Oh, this is my husband," or "I'd like to introduce you to my husband."

Although Joni and Friends was started by Joni, I feel that it's very much *my* ministry, as well. I don't feel like I'm overshadowed. I don't feel like I'm in a subservient role when Joni's on that platform. I think God has gifted Joni in very, very special ways. So I feel my position at that particular point is to be supportive. My leadership is in our home. So there's a nice mix right there.

And if you were to ask Joni, she would feel the same. In fact, it's interesting how we have meshed and molded into one, how we think alike. We're working together. It's kind of like we're one unit.

Q Is it sometimes hard for the two of you to have a private life because of your visibility?

A I wouldn't be honest if I didn't say at times, it's hard for Joni and me to have a private life. No matter where we go, the high visibility is there. I mean, when folks see an oriental and a blond girl in a wheelchair, it kind of stands out.

But we want to be sensitive to those folks who come up and greet us. For many of them, it's their first chance to talk with us. So we've come to the conclusion that when we're out in public, we are witnesses for God, that it's part of our ministry. We try to be as gracious and sensitive to these folks as possible.

Q There's been a lot of talk recently, Ken, about Joni's desire to have children. I assume you mean your own, and not adopted children.

A That's right. You know, interestingly enough, I don't think a lot of people realize that quadriplegia doesn't necessarily mean you can not have children. To make one blanket statement, people who are injured on the same level as Joni have different qualities. Their spinal column may have been severed in the same position, but some have more abilities to do things, and some have less. So in terms of having children, overall, I would have to say that quadriplegic folks, as well as paraplegics, often can have children.

Of course, I think it's important that a physician is consulted to find out what the possibility is of having a child. Joni and I have discussed this and have sought out professional opinions. It's their opinion we can try to have children. We'd be real excited if we had a child. But again, this is in prayer and we would appreciate your prayers for us. At this time, though, my wife is not going to have a baby.

Q Of course, the care of any children would entail a lot of work for both of you.

A That's true. But I don't have any negative feelings about the fact that I might be washing floors, or vacuuming, or dusting if we had a baby—things we perhaps have labelled should be done by women. I don't really feel there's a dividing line between what men and women should do in terms of running a house or caring for a child.

Now it scares me to think about the responsibilities involved in that. But if we have children, I think, God, again, would give us the grace to work out these kinds of unique situations.

We've thought it out. It's the same as marriage, as with becoming a Christian. You get to a certain point, and then you take that step of faith.

I don't think either of us, never having had children, understands all the responsibilities and ramifications of what it means to become a parent. But we certainly both love children. And if God blesses us with a child, then I think He also would give us the grace, guidance, and wisdom to be good parents—as long as we're looking to Him.

I Remember the Great San Francisco Earthquake
by Janet Bollinger

My grandmother, who refers to herself as "the tough old bird," can date the change in her character to the year 1906. This was the year of the Great San Francisco Earthquake and the year she began to depend on God. She was 19, a demure and proper young lady, sheltered by her family in the very heart of San Francisco.

Today, when Grandmother recites the story of the Great San Francisco Earthquake her voice rises in pitch and her cheeks turn a soft pink. Grandmother is proud to have survived the earthquake and thankful that she learned quickly to depend on the Lord for courage and strength.

"During the shaking of that earthquake," she always begins, "death was right at my door. I prayed hard that day that God would spare my life. Well, he did. I survived. Many others did not.

Grandmother always pauses here as if thanking God for her long life. "I remember," she continues, "being awakened from my sleep at dawn by the tremors. My bed was rocking and I heard a rumbling—like thunder. I jumped out of bed and made my way across a shaky floor to the door and into the hall.

"My three brothers and two sisters were screaming and crying and Mama, the only calm one, herded us all into her room. Once we were all accounted for, Mama said, 'All right. Keep calm. Kneel by my bed—all of you—and let's pray.'

"The rumbling outside grew louder. Suddenly we heard Mama's china cabinet crash to the floor with all her lovely dishes.

"A lamp across Mama's bedroom hit the floor—then our canary's cage. I wanted to get up and see if our canary was all right. But I couldn't move. I just prayed harder. I was sure that at any minute the ground would open up and we'd all be gone. Who but God could help us?

"As suddenly as it began, the earthquake was over—the rumbling, the shaking, the awful power we felt all around us.

"I got up from my knees slowly, testing the floor. It didn't move. My sister had reached our canary and was crying. I knew he was dead.

"I moved to the window and looked on the destruction of San Francisco. The street was a mass of bricks and rubble, and people shouting and clawing their way through it all. A wagon with horses and a driver was caught in a huge crack in the middle of the road.

"I stood there in shock until I heard Mama shouting for Papa. Then we were all running to the bakery, Papa's place of business, in front of our house facing Hayes Street.

"God, let Papa be alive," I prayed as I ran stumbling over books lamps and broken glass.

"We found Papa standing in the middle of the bakery. His face was drawn and pale and he moved toward us as if in a daze. 'You're all right,' he said. 'Thank God, you're all right.'

"Well, we thought the worst was behind us. But, it was yet

to come. Later that day a fire broke out in a building close by our home. A woman who lived on nearby Van Ness Avenue, tried to fry some ham and eggs. She didn't know that the chimney on her stove had been damaged by the quake. The water lines were destroyed by the quake, allowing the fire to engulf blocks of homes and businesses. Our home and bakery were burned to the ground.

"Our family had always lived quite well. We'd never been hungry before. Now we had nothing. We were thankful for a small tent furnished by the Federal government and set up in what is now Golden Gate Park.

"I would have fallen apart if it hadn't been for our Lord. That night as I lay on a blanket on the hard ground, I asked God to help me get through all this trouble.

"I remember telling God that I wasn't giving up. I knew my family had very little to give me now. It was just God and me. And, somehow, I didn't feel dependent on my family anymore. I felt strong and unafraid.

"Well, I went to work for the first time in my life. I had to. I had to eat! And, you know, my life, in so many ways, became exciting."

Grandmother always chuckles and smiles at this point in her story. "It's exciting," she says, "to see what you and God can do together."

Now, at 94, my grandmother has lost none of her independent spirit, and she still manages to catch me off guard with her quick wit and buffoonery.

Grandmother's straight posture and salt-and-pepper wig express her concern for an orderly appearance. Never does she appear without her pink lipstick and her beaded necklace that coordinate her attire. She greets and dismisses each day with the same determined attitude which she must have adopted when she first saw the ruins of the San Francisco Earthquake and which gained for her the title, "the tough old bird." This toughness stems from the strength she finds in the Lord. "The two of us can do anything," she says with a grin—and she believes it.

The Age of Twelve
by Timothy N. Boyd

One of the interesting aspects of the life of Christ is that information about his childhood is so scarce. Aside from the birth narratives, the only other picture we have of Jesus' youth is the account of his visit to Jerusalem at the age of twelve. Yet, it is of great significance that Luke should choose this one event from the "silent years" of Christ. At this crucial time Jesus, under Jewish law, passed from childhood to adult status.

Every culture sets a time at which they consider their children to move into adult responsibilities. In Jesus' day the Romans, for example, viewed their male children as coming to maturity sometime between the ages of fourteen and seventeen. The exact age was determined by the family, based on a variety of factors. As a new adult the boy was given the right to wear the all-white *toga virilis* (toga of manhood), which marked him as a full citizen of Rome. Greeks, on the other hand, regarded their young men at age eighteen as entering a period of preparation for adult status. At age twenty the Greek male assumed his position as a full citizen. The Jewish male also went through a period of transition from child to adult, but this transition was different from other contemporary cultures in two aspects: (1) The Jewish rites of passage occurred earlier in the life of the boy, and (2) they were dominated by the religious beliefs of Judaism.

In earlier times Israel focused on the age of twenty as the age of responsibility because at this age a man could bear arms (Num. 1). As time passed Israel began to emphasize the assumption of religious responsibilities as the passage to adulthood. By Roman times this age roughly corresponded with puberty. Therefore, twelve was the age of maturity not only for Jesus but for all Jewish boys of the time.

Preparation for this assumption of maturity began very early in a Jewish boy's life. The father began to prepare his son at the age of six or seven by instructing him in the tradition of Israel and the precepts of the Law. The boy also was enrolled in the local synagogue school where his father's teaching was reinforced. He was taught to read and write, using the Torah as the chief teaching tool. Having been thus prepared during his early years, the boy assumed his position as a man in Jewish society during his twelfth year. Becoming an adult entailed many rights and related responsibilities.

From a theological viewpoint, a Jewish male at this age was thought to become responsible for his own relationship with God. Before maturity a child's fate was tied to his father. The child was liable for the father's sins and benefitted from his father's merits. The father was totally responsible for the son's actions. Having come to adulthood he was liable for his own sins and was expected to generate his own merits. He was viewed as being able to control his own desires. This transition is demonstrated in the father's benediction, "Blessed be He who has taken the responsibility for this child's doing from me."

From a legal perspective the young man was now able to perform certain acts. For example, he was now considered old enough to be part of a *bet din,* or a court of law. He also could now buy and sell property. It was recognized, however, that one just entering manhood was not totally prepared for complete responsibility. For example, his testimony was not valid in regard to real estate because he was not viewed as being knowledgeable about such subjects.

Upon obtaining maturity, a young man also was expected to obey many of the cultic (worship) practices of the Jewish religion. One aspect of his adulthood that had both legal and cultic implications was the young man's right to make up the *minyam* —the quorum of ten males which was required to constitute a synagogue. Without the presence of a *minyam,* Jews were forced to limit their worship to private devotion rather than the communal services of the synagogue.

Also at this time in life, a boy's religious vows were considered to be valid. Vows were a predominant feature of Judaism in Jesus' day. The vow was a solemn promise made to God in which the individual promised to deprive himself of something as an act of devotion to God. A child could make vows, but the father could cancel those vows by following certain procedures. When the son reached maturity he was totally bound by his vows and the father could no longer intervene.

The age of maturity also brought with it the obligation to fast. As with vows, fast days were a prominent part of the Jewish religious scene during New Testament times. Fasting involved abstaining from food, drink, bathing, and sexual intercourse for the length of the fast. Before the twelfth year children were expected to participate in partial fasts in order to prepare them for the full fasting of adulthood. Customarily, a boy completed his first complete fast day during the twelfth year. Following the completion of his first fast the boy received a blessing from the elders.

Another obligation of coming to maturity was that the young

man attended the three most important feasts of the Jewish religious year: Passover, Feast of Weeks, and Feast of Booths or Tabernacles. Many scholars see the incident recorded in Luke (2:41-46) as Jesus' first official observation of the Passover, while others see this visit as a part of his preparation to assume these duties.

The prayer life of the young man was another area which called for added responsibility with the coming of maturity. The conscientious Jew structured his daily life around the practice of prayer. After reaching adulthood every male was required to put on the phylacteries and join in the daily morning prayers of faithful Jews. These phylacteries were small boxes made of leather which contained verses of Scripture. They were attached to the forehead and to the left arm using leather thongs. These devices served to remind the adult Jewish male of his obligations under the covenant.

One of the privileges associated with coming of age was being called to the front of the synagogue to read from the Torah. This was done on the first occasion after the thirteenth birthday to demonstrate publicly that the boy had now assumed his full participation in the covenant. He was now fully a "son of the Law." The reading of Scripture was a central feature of synagogue worship, and thus by reading before the synagogue the young man's new position within the religious community was graphically demonstrated.

When Jesus' parents discovered him in the Temple talking with the elders, he told them that he had to be about his Father's business. It would seem from his remarks that Jesus himself was very aware of his new status within Judaism. After this encounter, Jesus returned home with Joseph and Mary to continue maturing and preparing for his ministry. Although not all of the aspects of childhood were gone, at the age of twelve he became a full member of the covenant people.

Reach Out and Write Someone
by Carol C. Crawford

Day after day, the newspaper tells us we're becoming a nation of gypsies. One story said that every week last year, one thousand people moved into Dallas as five hundred people simultaneously moved out. We constantly pack and unpack furniture, children, and memories. But we can't pack up and take with us the friends we leave behind at each stop.

Maybe that's why I can't bring myself to throw away old letters. They're more than accounts of births and weddings and job changes. Like old friends, they offer counsel, minister to the miseries of homesickness, and maintain lifelines of communication while I'm away from friends. Unlike the telephone, they're permanent proof that I have a place in the lives and affections of others.

So I hang on to the note from my mother telling me not to join the Air Force without asking her first. And the letter my sister wrote advising me to get a dog to help fill up my lonely apartment. And the card from a California friend saying *of course* I should take the new job. Those decisions are long past, but the written words show me that I still have people to turn to for understanding and guidance.

At certain times in history, letters are even more crucial. Imprisoned by the Nazis, theologian Dietrich Bonhoeffer carried on what correspondence he could with his family and close friends. He describes the joy their letters brought him:

> It is as though the prison gates were opened for a moment, and I could share a little of your life outside.

One Letter at a Time

Knowing how much enjoyment letters bring should inspire us to pick up a pen. But writing letters takes time many of us think we don't have. Here are some tried and true ideas for finding the time and making the best use of it. . . .

A busy graduate student I know has worked out a painless way to get letters into her schedule. As soon as she's read her mail, she sorts it into two piles. One pile contains letters she'll answer when it's convenient; the other holds those that need immediate answers, like a request for someone's address or a recipe. These two stacks go, rubber-banded, into a drawer. "They depress me when they're out all over the desk waiting for me," she says.

Next, she looks for *small* segments of time, (such as the ten minutes before the potatoes are done) and pulls out *one letter at a time* to reply.

"People think they have to carve out a whole morning to answer *all* their mail," she says. "Then they never get to it. Taking one at a time is more realistic and more fun."

To take advantage of other spare moments when you're not at home, keep four or five stamps and a few notecards in your purse. Some brands of small stationery are sold in plastic packets so they can survive burial under lipstick and car keys. If your address list is a pocket-size one, it can go along too. Thus equipped, you're ready to take advantage of a lunch hour or a long wait at the dentist's office.

Postcards of small folded notes are more appealing than large sheets of stationery, because you know you won't have to write an epic to fill them. "People just want to hear from you," one friend said. "You don't have to write a book."

Conversations on Paper

Sometimes the problem isn't finding the time. It's deciding what to say and where to start. Writing comes easier when you can remember that it's a form of conversation. By sharing more feelings than facts, you may brighten someone's day and given him or her a keepsake as well. If the blank stationery sheet brings on panic instead of ideas, give yourself a *specific* purpose for the letter even before you start, such as . . .

Encouragement. Amid my stacks of letters from 1974 is one from a college roommate, addressed to me at my new summer job at a girls' camp. It begins simply: "I thought you might need some encouragement at this point." (She was right!) She then proceeded to catalogue specific things I had done well at school the year before. The letter closed with Jer. 32:27, "Behold, I am the Lord, the God of all flesh. Is anything too hard for me?"

Praise. The minister of education in an Alabama church decided to write a personal thank you to all her Vacation Bible School workers a few years ago. The notes were a long time in coming, she said, because there were a great many women involved. But I like to imagine the pleasure and surprise of those summer-weary volunteers when they realized someone *did* appreciate their gallons of lemonade and endless craft projects.

Counsel. Offering advice when no one's asked for it can be risky. But love involves counsel, especially between parent and child or between intimate friends. Good-natured questions have a familiar ring to them that is a comfort. A friend wants to know how my exercise program is going. Dad wants to know if I've taken on too much of a workload. They're reminders that our relationships haven't changed, that even 400 miles away, parents are entitled to ask if you're eating right.

Consolation. Although so greatly needed, these can be the most difficult notes to begin. We don't much like to think about suffering, and we often don't know quite what to say to those going through it. A few who have been there tell me that simple and short messages are best, such as "I'm thinking about you—I know it's a difficult time for you." A simple card with a verse and your name may be sufficient. Knowing that you don't have to offer an explanation or a sermon may encourage you to write.

Long-Distance Concern. There are dozens of creative ways to approach your correspondence. One faraway friend saved all her Christmas cards in a special file. Beginning in January, she took out one card each day during her early morning devotional. After praying for that person or family, she wrote them a short note to say she'd been thinking of them.

"That kind of discipline keeps me writing," she said. "Otherwise it's the kind of thing you let slip by." She had so much fun following this system, she soon had to discipline herself to write only one letter a day!

As the lucky recipient of one of those notes, I can attest to the joy of being remembered and affirmed by one I haven't seen face-to-face in quite a few years.

As a small child, I was privileged to receive letters from my grandfather, each a masterpiece of ingenuity. One letter began at the center of the page, with the words winding around each other in a spiral, so that you had to turn the page around and around to read it. Sometimes he would begin a letter to me on one line, a letter to my sister on the next, and continue to alternate lines on each page. Once he used a different color ink for almost every word, and sometimes he would use crazy stationery, like adding machine tape, all to our great delight.

He's gone now, and the letters are somewhere in the dark recesses of the attic, perhaps beyond reclamation. Still, memory has framed them as bright capsules of time and thought devoted exclusively to his grandchildren, despite the miles that separated us. They are almost like photographs, if such a thing were possible, of creativity and love.

Full and familiar as we try to make them, these little envelopes that follow us from zip code to zip code can't do everything. They can't bring friends to us in person or return us to an old neighborhood we loved. But perhaps they will ease the transition a little, offering handwritten hugs where human arms can't reach.

Death Valley Quiet Times
by Tim Cummings

Craggy, arthritic sandstone figures jut out of the seemingly endless sea of sand. Windswept dunes change shape like slow-moving clouds. Sand, wind and sun angrily buffet any life persistent enough to reside in the desert. And . . . well, you get the idea. Deserts on the average are dry places and not well liked by the general public. Even our vocabulary is unkind to arid places. We call them *waste* lands or *bad* lands or Death Valley.

Sometimes I open my Bible and hear the hollow, formless wind of the desert eroding my enthusiasm to read Scripture. The voice that reads to me in my head goes monotone, slows down and sometimes whispers, "This is boring." Then I ask myself if reading a Christian comic book would count as having a Quiet Time.

The erosion continues. Not only is Scripture dry, but prayer becomes anhydrous. Soon I am bickering with Christians about stupid things. I am on my way to becoming a craggy, arthritic, sandstone Christian.

Boredom is a hard enemy to fight because we cannot see it. Where does it come from? Must I just wait for it to go away,

or can I do something to fight it? As with the water beneath the
desert, we need to probe beneath that crusty, lifeless boredom
to find the cool, life-giving water of the Word. Here are some
things I have learned from my occasional Death Valley Quiet
Times.

Cold Symptoms

Many times when the Bible goes bad on us, it is a symptom
of something else in our life which is not right. Check it out.
Is it dorm food? Bad mood? Relationship on the rocks? Too
little sleep? GPA blues? Test anxiety? Sin? No one has un-
plugged your Bible. So first check *your* connections.

Then cultivate a relationship with the Bible. Exploration is
a key in reading. When I have been taken on an adventure by
means of a book, I sense an odd sort of friendship with it. C.
S. Lewis fans talk about Narnia as if they have invested in real
estate there. They've gone on an adventure. It can be that way
with the Bible.

After attending an Inter-Varsity conference on inductive
Bible study, I came home and began tearing into 1 Corinthians.
I told myself there would be nothing in that book that I would
not understand. I explored the book. It became *my* book. Even
five years later I have a sense of ownership toward 1 Corinthians.

The psalmist wrote of such a relationship in Psalm 119. Just
look at the words he uses to describe his relationship with
Scripture. Attitudes: I will treasure [thy precepts], have regard
for them, long for, wait for, esteem right, stand in awe, love, and
rejoice in them. Action: I will walk in, observe, seek, keep
diligently, look unto, learn, proclaim, meditate on, remember,
cleave to, not turn aside from, turn my feet toward, believe in,
diligently consider, perform, and sing of thy law. Each phrase

becomes a challenge and a goal for me in my growing relationship with Scripture.

How can we build the psalmist's words into our own relationship with the Bible? I have extracted five principles from my own experience.

Principle 1: Pray for desire. I was a second-year Bible-college student when I spoke with a friend about how short and dry my Bible studies had been. Wayne began telling me of some guys he knew in western Canada who had "stacks and stacks" of Bibles so severely worn, underlined and color-coded that they could hardly be read. "Sometimes they spend eight hours a day just studying Scripture!" It didn't matter if he was speaking in hyperbole or not. What mattered was that my Quiet Times had bottomed out. But I wanted to have stacks and stacks of mentally digested Bibles. I wanted to pore over Scripture for hours on end.

So I prayed. I told God my problem with boredom. He answered. But not in one big zap. I spent some time thinking about the place of Scripture in God's whole scheme of revealing himself. It is somewhat startling that the Creator has left us a diary of his activities and accomplishments! Through the pages of the Bible we learn what God likes and dislikes. We see him at work in the lives of various people and nations. We come to grips with his character. We learn the significance of the life of Christ, of the cross and of the empty tomb. Boring? My casual attitude toward the Bible had ended. I converted to the idea that Scripture had to be central in my life.

But you can have a good attitude toward the Bible and still find it boring at times. That's why this article doesn't end here.

Principle 2: Start somewhere. Begin! What book in the Bible would be intriguing to read now? Pick a starting place. I have found that my driest times are when I'm between books. I don't know what to study next or what method to use. So I either read bits and pieces indifferently or lose my desire to read at all.

The key to this is quite simple. Have a book chosen and a study method ready when you end your current study. What books do you know the least about? Look for questions or interesting issues in your current study. Maybe these will naturally lead you to the next book. For example, while studying the book of Hebrews, I got interested in the Old Testament priesthood. So my next book was Leviticus. While in Leviticus, I found myself in the middle of the story, so I decided to study the five books of Moses (Genesis to Deuteronomy). I wasn't able to stop until I finished Joshua and Judges. I didn't have to worry about a starting place for five months!

Principle 3: Variety. Put a little schizophrenia into your study. Change versions, methods, Testaments, even the place where you study. Part of the adventure of Bible study is in how we approach our task. Too much routine can breed boredom. If you know exactly what and exactly how you are going to study five years from now, you're in for it. Variety will help you stay out of the desert.

Principle 4: Use your strengths. If you have a knack for organizing ideas, then theme studies or book outlines will work with your natural inclinations. If you are creative with words, maybe making up titles for paragraphs and chapters will be enjoyable. Perhaps you like to write. Try keeping a journal or writing your own devotional. I spent a month with ten verses in this way and had a great time. If you're the inquisitive type, write seven questions about each chapter and answer them. A key to good study is knowing how to ask questions. You may also want to graph or illustrate what you read. If you are good at telling stories, try rewriting (or taping) some of the narratives of Scripture. You will find Bible study much more enjoyable if you use abilities you already possess.

Principle 5: Have something in your hand when it's over. One of my most cherished possessions is a green three-ring notebook which contains almost five years' worth of various (and I mean *various*) types of studies I've done. I have used it as a resource on many occasions. Parts of it are typed, others are scrawled. Much of it is multicolored.

Writing things down in study helps me to focus my thinking. Even when I am trying to cover lots of territory (like Genesis through Deuteronomy), I can pause long enough to think of the main thought in a chapter and jot a title down. Today could be the start of a cherished three-ring notebook for you.

Guidelines

We are safer if we leash our imaginations so our Bible studies do not run amuck. Don't be afraid to go a little wild and crazy, but always bring your ideas to bear on these five guidelines:

1. Am I absorbing content? Keep your focus on God's truth as you study. It is possible to give your attention to the exercise rather than its purpose. Be a good steward of his truth.

2. Am I drawing application? After you have understood a passage, make sure you bring it to bear on your life. Without this guideline, you are like the fool who built his house on sand. Even questions like "What has Moses got that I haven't?" can open up ideas of application for you.

3. Am I communing with God? Bible study can be an exercise in creativity, or a sort of mental feast. But it is not an end in itself. Your goal in Bible study is God himself. It is possible to ignore God while reading Scripture. Don't.

4. Have I come to the Bible to be changed? This attitude dovetails with the second guideline. Are you thirsty for righteousness? Will you allow God's Word to guide your personality and lifestyle?

5. Am I a student? A student approaches his teaching material with humility. Using the Bible to prove our points of view or forcing it to say what it does not say are very poor ways to learn. "Teach me thy ways; show me thy paths" should be the prayer on our lips as we humbly sit at the feet of our Lord.

Some Methods I Have Loved

A variety of methods can rescue you from boredom. Allow me to quickly catalogue my top nine.

1. Inductive Bible study. This method is fairly involved, but worth the effort. In three major steps—observation, interpretation, application—you boil down the basic principles of the text. It involves observing grammatical connections, marking sections of a passage, titling paragraphs, and writing questions. (The whole layout would make another article.) Inter-Varsity offers a training weekend in this method called Bible and Life Level 2. This method is intricate and time-consuming. As usual, the best is the hardest.

2. Paragraph and chapter titles. This method will help you center on main points in Scripture. It can also be a fun way to remember what goes on in a certain passage. Can you guess where these passages are? "Tablets' Second Printing; Rash Measures for Skin Disease; Here's Mud in Your Eye; Warning for Wilderness Christians." Simply list in your notebook a title for every paragraph you study, and then an overall title for the chapter.

3. Theme study. I bought a Bible to use exclusively for this method. Each theme is color-coded with pencils. Then I trace recurrent themes in various books by underlining the passage in the appropriate color. For instance, in my Bible all the passages in the Gospel of John having something to do with the deity of Christ are underlined in orange. Other themes might be life, belief or signs. Themes in Jeremiah include chronology, reasons for judgment, idolatry, remnant and God's refusal to hear. Find your own. This method can get exciting—I sometimes skipped class to do it!

4. Titles and themes. This combines the second and third methods. Instead of underlining in a Bible, you underline in your notebook the titles of the paragraphs which contain a recurring theme. (Repetition shows emphasis on something important.)

5. Book overview chart. Chapters are titled. Then, depending on the nature of the book, add more graphs or maps. Mark off larger sections of the book as you notice three or four major turning points. For Genesis, I added a list of the meanings of some of the names. You may wish to elaborate by finding key verses or the central theme of the book. My Joshua chart has a map of the progression which Israel made through the Promised Land. Judges has a chart which tells how long Israel was in bondage under different governments.

6. Write your own devotional. Keep a journal of your own thoughts as you study a passage. But beware of spiritualizing every pebble in the brook or bird in the sky. Some published devotionals get away with murdering the text. Stay true to the truth. Incidentally, John White suggested this method in *The Fight* (IVP), so it must be a good idea.

7. Read a short book several times. Occasionally I get burned out on writing anything down. A few years back I decided to read the entire book of Colossians every morning for five days. A friend of mine who's a pastor read 1 Peter every day for a month. You'll be amazed at the insights gleaned from this concentrated survey.

8. Write and answer seven questions on each chapter. You might ask why Matthew divides the genealogy into three sets of fourteen. Or what qualities Paul demonstrates as a discipler in 1 Thessalonians 2. I spent a week in 1976 chasing down Paul's thorn in the flesh. Although I didn't find a conclusive answer, I still remember the various speculations I ran across during my quest. Be merciless on yourself with questions, but balance that with asking the obvious.

9. *Rewrite or retell.* Narratives, parables and Cecil B. DeMille events in Scripture lend themselves well to storytelling. For ideas, look for a book about how to tell stories, read a children's Bible, or read stories by good authors. (I'm always nosing through the Arthurian legends for pure fun, and for tips.)

I mentioned earlier the psalmist's relationship to Scripture. Psalm 119 also tells us what effects we can expect from God's Word. Our way becomes steadfast, we are kept pure, our weary soul is strengthened, our reverence for God increases. We gain wisdom, peace, stability and integrity. We can answer when we are taunted. The list goes on.

God's Word can be an adventure. It is not *always* fun. I still have week-long dry spells with Death Valley Quiet Times. But eventually the water of the Word surfaces, and things come alive again. God will draw you nearer to himself through creative, enjoyable study of his Word.

Changing Their World:
An Interview with Tony and Lois Evans
by Carol M. Dettoni

"I've always felt there needs to be a new face for the black church—new wine skins, so to speak," Tony stated. "It's been an uphill climb because a lot of the things we are talking about historically are not a part of the black community. We don't want to lose a lot of things that are intrinsically a part of our community, but we want to bring a new kind of direction. We want to cause black churches to look at their traditions and determine which ones are for today."

How did Tony and Lois get such a vision for ministry in the black community? Lois, poised and attractive with a soft British accent, was born and raised in a devout Christian family of ten in Guyana, South America. Tony, winsomely modest, articulate and obviously athletic, grew up a continent away in Baltimore, Maryland. It was when Tony participated in an evangelistic crusade in Guyana that he and Lois met.

"My dad was on the committee for the crusade," Lois recalled. "He met Tony at the airport and invited him to dinner. We saw, after talking together, that we had the same interest in ministry." After Lois and Tony married, they continued holding crusades and evangelistic meetings, eventually moving to Dallas, Texas where Tony received his theological training and doctoral degree at Dallas Theological Seminary. Significant things happened in their lives: They were challenged to the pastoral ministry and the first two of their children were born—Crystal, now 10 years old, and Priscilla, 7. Anthony, 4, and year-old Jonathon have since joined the family.

For the past six years Tony has served as pastor of the Oak Cliff Bible Fellowship, a growing, integrated church in Dallas, as well as Bible study teacher for the Mavericks basketball and Cowboys football teams. In addition, Tony teaches at Dallas Theological Seminary, is vice-president of Pro Basketball Fellowship, vice-president of the National Black Evangelical Association, and is vice-president of Black Evangelistic Enterprises (BEE), an organization involved in church planting and assisting black churches throughout the country in evangelism, literature distribution, radio ministry, home Bible studies and ministries to youth and college students.

"The pastoral ministry was the last thing we wanted to do," Tony acknowledged. "Full-time evangelism is what I had given my life to—holding crusades and small meetings." But during seminary Tony became aware of the acute need for strong biblical teaching, particularly in the black community. That new awareness raised Tony's interest in the pastoral ministry and he was encouraged to start a new church. He has found that being a pastor allows him the opportunity to put into action some of his innovative ideas for serving God in the black community. "And I'm still involved in evangelism," he said, "so that area of my life is fulfilled."

Ministry has been an everyday habit for Tony since he was a child. "My father was involved in Christian work on a daily basis. When Dad went to witness, I would be there. When he was on the corner handing out tracts, I would be there." Living with that model every day made a lifetime impression on Tony. He loved and played football, and was drafted by a professional team; but being successful in sports did not have the same impact on him as being involved with what his father was doing. "The Lord was the theme of our house—everything exemplified the Lord," Tony added.

Tony and Lois are following their parents' lead in making the Lord Jesus central to their family life. "I think family devotions are mandatory," Tony said. "On Mondays I have a little Bible study with the girls." He has taken the subject of baptism, going over it in preparation for their own baptismal experiences and giving them home assignments to complete.

Scripture memorization is also important in the Evans family. "Around the dinner table or just before bed we each say a favorite Scripture that we've learned," Lois shared. "We do a lot of that. And we sometimes tell stories and then act them out or pantomime them, which is fun."

Although she is active in the life of the church—overseeing a monthly Bible study, taking part in the music ministry, helping in the child learning center—Lois takes seriously the advice she has received from others: children grow so quickly and time spent with them is vital. "The (church) ministry is important and very demanding," Lois noted, "but I think for me, right now, my children are my ministry."

Time for each other is most important to Lois and Tony. "We try to take half a weekend away (Friday and Saturday) once a month," Tony commented. "I'm probably home four out of seven evenings. All of my business meetings at the church are scheduled on the first Saturday of the month so that I can be home the other three. And I take Mondays off, too."

Horseback riding, swimming and skating—"We're crazy about skating," Lois said—are the family's favorite activities.

"And Tony enjoys playing basketball," she added. "When I can't find him or the children, they're playing basketball."

Tony's obvious commitment to his wife and four children melds with a deep commitment to upholding biblical principles in the various facets of his ministry. And discussing the cultural, social and spiritual needs of the black community is a subject about which Tony very quickly becomes animated and excited.

One of Tony's first challenges as a pastor was the implementation of expository preaching in the black pulpit. "Black preaching has typically been topical (in approach)," he stated. "And that's not all bad. In fact, to a large extent, it's been good." But he added that there is a great need for more Bible teaching and more Christian education in the black church.

Tony's church is also attempting to develop a constituency of church people whose life-styles will reflect the doctrines that are being taught. "There is a lot of criticism among blacks in regard to the lack of models," he said. "In the community where people live we want to present models of families who can really make a difference spiritually."

One of Tony's chief concerns in this area of modeling is that men take more responsibility in the raising of their families. "There's an understood delegation from men to women in the family," Tony said. "Some of that is necessary because the man is responsible for breadwinning. I think to a large extent it's an excuse to get out of a primary obligation stated in Scripture— men are to be models and leaders in their homes to their families. This needs to happen, particularly in the black community."

While Tony acknowledges that social issues are of major concern in the black community, his burden is for social action that operates from a biblical basis and will thus have lasting results. In an effort to provide that kind of practical care for the needy as well as offer a unique opportunity for evangelism, Oak

Cliff Bible Fellowship sets aside time in the morning and evening services for people to share their needs and hurts. Before a person walks out of the church, most of his physical needs will have been met through the church pantry or through other members of the fellowship. "We're trying to teach our church families to meet the needs of other families so that they become accountable to one another," Tony noted. "One of the things we feel strongly is that the church as a community is not a place you visit on Sunday, but it is a community of people who share, care, love and die for one another."

A preschool child care center in the educational building of the church offers another avenue of practical evangelism. "When a preschooler comes, we send an evangelistic team to the home to share with the parents what we're doing in the center—which is strongly academic and strongly Christian," Tony said. "And we have an opportunity to share why we're doing it—Jesus Christ."

Integrated ministries for Lois and Tony, both at church and through their home, have offered opportunities to break down racial barriers. And, according to Tony, it is in the home that racial prejudice must first be confronted. "The most practical way to face racial prejudice must first be confronted. "The most practical way to face racial prejudice is for parents to make sure they've dealt with their own prejudices first, because if they haven't it will either be communicated subtly or directly to the children." And then broadening the sphere of relationships is important. "That's where the church, the body of Christ, is so crucial," he continued. "Churches do not have to be integrated but they certainly should be related to each other, black and white, because we're all part of one body." For example, the Oak Cliff Bible Fellowship is working very closely with a predominantly white church in North Dallas. "We're like brother and sister churches," Tony stated. "We're working on a strategy to minister to the community, mutually helping one another."

Are Tony and Lois Evans really revolutionaries? Perhaps not, but they are clearly breaking new ground in their ministry to the black community. "As far as the ministry is concerned, my pet word is alternative," Tony said. "The church of Jesus Christ is to provide an option for the world. We can't do that if we amalgamate into the world and we can't do that if we run from the world. We must be in the world but not of it. We must be an alternative to it."

How to Quarterback Your Own Education
by Bruce C. Dodd, Jr.

Can you imagine a quarterback who practices only when he feels like it, frequently runs to the wrong goal and calls, "Kill the clock!" in the middle of touchdown drives? As ridiculous as it sounds, classroom quarterbacks make these painful mistakes every day. No wonder they fail to see school as great sport.

Students today have more freedom to choose their goals and how to reach them than ever before in the history of American education. A powerful team of both amateurs and professionals respond to the signals they are given.

"What can we do?" concerned parents ask. The media bombards educators for their failures, students and teachers complain about each other and everyone too often suffers in noisy desperation. It's time to call for quiet in the huddle and get the team together.

Unfortunately, there has been a strange conspiracy of silence concerning five critical aspects of the school game plan.

1. **For more than twenty-five years the parent team members have been benched in many schools.** "We are the experts," professional school-persons assert, "let us handle the prob-

---

From *Family Life Today,* Oct. 1983. © Copyright 1983 by *Family Life Today,* 1550 Elizabeth St., Pasadena, CA 91104. Used by permission.

lems." Timid and unsure parents who sense trouble have remained silent. The verbally affluent and often factually poor parents inevitably compound the problems by being wrong at the top of their voices. As a remedy, model schools have produced parent handbooks, held open forums and workshops, and prevented problems by not letting them develop. Draining the swamp is easier than fighting the alligators. Willing parent resource and support persons are available in almost all communities. Failing to use them is like walking ten miles to work when you have a new car in the garage. Strangest of all is the student's failure to see his/her own parents as members of the education team. Instead they are often viewed as fans of the opponents.

2. **Students inhibit themselves academically by assuming that their education is a product of their school rather than of themselves.** At best a person's education is a 50/50 agreement in which the school provides the teaching half and the student supplies the learning half. Families that see schools as primarily social institutions or treat them as such are in for a catch-up education game in the final period. Students who approach teachers on an "us versus them" basis may not understand the next play before they leave the huddle. Frankly, a good teacher and a successful student may not be friends, but *they must not be enemies.*

3. **Some of the basic skills of the game have been overlooked in the rush to answer "What's new in education?"** Productive scholars and business executives spend half their time listening. With the contemporary emphasis on reading, listening is taken for granted and is seldom taught as a skill. With the help of university researchers, industry discovered at least ten common obstacles to good listening. Some of them even seem to be good habits. For example: trying to remember all the facts in a passage or presentation is hopeless. Facts tend to stick to the ideas they support. Consequently, students need to focus on ideas—

not facts. Minds are like closets. Without hooks, hangers and shelves, clothes must be rescued at random from a heap. Information, too, needs to be put away properly for easy recall reference.

Since listening is a skill, it can be taught. Rudyard Kipling wrote,

> "I have six honest serving men.
> They taught me all I know.
> Their names are Who and What
>   and When
> And Where and Why and How."

Kipling's six honest serving men work for successful students. They provide the hooks, hangers and shelves in the mind for storing key information. Listening may be the lost art of modern classrooms. Unlike the dropkick of yesterday's football, good listening was never replaced with a better way.

4. Perhaps it is the person within the existing student who needs the most help. Almost everyone suffers from an inadequate self-image. Ideal students believe in themselves and cope with the classroom on an "I can" basis. Dr. Edward de Bono, who directs England's Center for the Study of Thinking, says, "In teaching thinking (to the young) the basic benefit has been to change their self-image from the either-or poles of 'I am intelligent/not intelligent' to 'I am a thinker.' It's a fundamental change in the way (they) think about themselves . . . they're engaged in a process at which they feel they can get better and better."

Mark Twain once observed, "Nothing so needs reforming as other people's habits." Perhaps the adult can avoid the hypocrisy involved in attempting to manipulate others by seeking to influence students as a coach. Coaches and their teams have well-defined common goals.

Those who know the education game understand the critical responsibility of saying forthrightly that certain patterns of learning and study behavior are vastly superior to others. No one needs a dictator, but students could use some effective coaching at home and in school. Most students need to be shown that they can find half the questions to the next history quiz in 10 minutes *before* they read the assigned pages. A simple study skill usually called "Survey and Question" does the trick in those critical 10 minutes.

5. By the time a student reaches high school, most teachers teach subjects, not the most effective ways to learn those subjects. Their courses are occasions to use good study skills—not learn them. Accordingly, *a student must devise a suitable method of study for each class,* founded on motives that are self-provided and self-evaluated.

This article will not replace a good handbook on study skills, but it does provide the same kind of information a quarterback requests from his spotter in the stands. Where are the main problems? What type of plays will work?

The tide of the education game turns dramatically but silently when a student seizes three great thoughts:

1. I am a young person with the primary occupation of student—not just a kid with an obligation to go to school.

2. Success in school will make me happy, since all five measurable elements of happiness in students are related to school achievement.

3. I was born to win—especially in school since learned skills, positive attitudes and hard work are the keys to success.

The game is only a metaphor, but there is a potential touchdown in every well-executed play. The metaphor is useful if it helps young people to grow in wisdom and stature and in favor with God and humanity.

Nowhere Else to Go
by Donnie Galloway

Mile after lonely mile, I kept thinking of my cousin. The thoughts were submerged, hidden down deep; and I tried not to pay them any mind. I talked on my CB some, read all the signs for Stuckey's and Fieldcrest and furniture outlets posted on U.S. Interstate 85, stopped off for a bite to eat at Darrell's Barbecue in Rockwell, North Carolina.

But, like a magnet, my mind kept coming back to my cousin. We'd been close, he and I. Two weeks before, he had killed himself. His suicide stunned me, and inside I felt a heaviness, like a weight, tight, in my chest.

Sad and puzzled, I remembered back to some of those times we'd hung around together. We'd talked for hours, about this or that. He was young. Life was before him, but . . .

Death. We'd never talked about that.

It had been raining off and on, and the grayness of the day seemed to play on my mind. I was driving south, hauling a load of bricks from Lewis Run, Pennsylvania, to Baton Rouge, Louisiana. It was 1982; and I'd been running heavy freight for 10 years, ever since I was 18.

As the 1972 Brockway truck and I pushed into my home

territory of North Carolina, those thoughts of death traveled with me. I remembered grimly that I hadn't even been able to go to his funeral. My mother had to tell me about it. The company I drove for then wouldn't let me off. And I'd been asked to be a pall bearer.

It was sprinkling as I pulled out of the weigh station south of Charlotte. I was about to undergo a great change. If only my cousin had still been alive and riding with me that day. His life might have changed, just as mine did.

Just ahead was the Catawba River Bridge, a span of 175 yards. As I drove onto the bridge, an orange sign announced: "Right lane closed—1000 feet ahead." I waited for a lady in a small car to pass, then I pulled over into the left lane behind her.

Suddenly, right in front of me, all of the cars had stopped. But I couldn't! Five tons of metal and 11 tons of bricks were going to smash right into all those people. *Oh, no, dear God, I'm going to kill all of them!* my mind screamed.

There's nowhere else to go, I thought desperately, pulling the wheel hard to the right. In a split second, I knew I had to drive off the bridge. It was either that or kill everyone in front of me.

As I swerved and drove to the edge of the bridge, I heard metal crash into metal. Then I was through the guard rail and falling . . . the truck and the bricks and I plunging 80 feet through the air. I was terrified. *This is it!*

We hit the river hard, and the windshield burst. Muddy water gushed in and swept me back into the sleeper. The truck sank the 35 feet to the river bottom in a hurry. I was dazed, and my sleeping gear and tools and everything I owned floated around me, confusing me. I couldn't see.

I groped through the blackness. My clothes and boots felt like lead. My lungs were about to burst. I'd never get out of there.

I touched the steering wheel. Beyond was the open windshield and I struggled to it just as the truck began flipping over in a slow arc. Soon my opening would be lying against the river bottom, and I'd be trapped.

I kicked and pushed. I pulled myself through. But then I was lost. I felt as if I were in a tomb, surrounded by choking blackness. Which way was up? I didn't know. I just stretched out my arms and swam.

And then my head hit the river bottom. That's when I gave up. I did say some prayers. It was my time to die.

"Dear God, if You want me to live, or if You want me to die, please go with me. And, dear God, help those people on the bridge. Don't let anyone be hurt. *Please.*"

I gave up to whatever was going to happen. And I didn't feel afraid anymore.

Then I felt my body lifting up . . . *and up and up*—10 feet, 20, 30, 35. I was being *pushed* up. I broke onto the surface, and there was a boat with two fishermen motoring toward me!

I gasped and choked and hollered, and went under a couple of times, but I fought my way back to the top. I was still *alive!* I fought to stay afloat until those fishermen grabbed me and pulled me into their boat.

I lay on the bottom of the boat gasping and coughing, gulping in small breaths of air. It felt good, breathing in life again.

Then I managed to say, "Did I hurt anyone? Is everyone okay?"

We looked up at the bridge deck. There were flashing lights. Troopers and wreckers. Crowds of people looking down at us. I gulped. There was an ambulance. *Somebody must have gotten hurt bad,* I thought. For just a second, living didn't feel so good anymore.

The two men with me in the boat yelled up to the bridge, asking if anyone else was hurt. Then I heard the answering voice. "Everybody's okay up here. We called an ambulance for the trucker."

"How is the trucker?" someone shouted from the bridge.

"A bit winded, but he's in pretty good shape!"

Good shape. Well, one of my legs may never be the same, and my back gives me some trouble now, but I'm still hauling heavy loads on an 18-wheeler flatbed truck. And I still drive sometimes over the Catawba River Bridge. There's a patch in the guard rail where I drove through that day, and that patch reminds me of the lesson I learned down on the bottom of that river. I learned something special about life.

I learned it while I was facing death. I knew down there that I would never be afraid of death, but I also discovered something else, something that my cousin could have learned, but didn't: You don't need to be afraid of *life,* either. Because if you'll just reach out and ask God to go with you, He'll lift you up and walk with you the rest of the way.

God has a purpose for each one of us. He wants us to live, and He'll give us the courage to live, if we just give Him the chance.

The Little Things You May Not Hear
by Lin Grensing

The spoken word is a major mode of communication—yet it is by no means the only one. Nonverbal communications also plays a vital role in our interaction with others.

The most common types of nonverbal communication are familiar to us all. A nod of the head, a wave of the hand, a frown—each of these conveys a message.

For instance:

While Joan is telling her husband about the dinner party she is planning for the weekend, he has folded his arms across his chest and is gazing at the floor with a slight frown. Is Joan going to get the impression that he is excited about it?

Christmas morning finds Brian and Jenny racing eagerly into the living room, eyes wide and smiles lighting up their young faces. Will their parents assume that they are dreading the moment when they are to open their gifts?

Though the importance of *verbal* communication cannot be denied, it is also important to watch for *non*verbal cues. Always verify your perceptions of another person's nonverbal message, however, to avoid misunderstandings.

From *Seek,* 18 Mar. 1984. © Copyright 1984 by Standard Publishing, 8121 Hamilton Ave., Cincinnati, OH 45231. Used by permission.

Our entire body is utilized when we speak. Body language has become a frequently discussed issue these days, with many theories offering their interpretations of certain gestures and body movements.

It is important to note, however, that not only do nonverbal behaviors differ with each person and situation, but evidence suggests that the connotations of these behaviors also vary among cultures.

To understand the importance of nonverbal communication in our interaction with others, consider the following:

• Are there certain gestures which you commonly use to illustrate a point?

• Can you effectively send a message of disapproval to your children with just a glance?

• How closely do you stand to those you like? To those you dislike?

We all send nonverbal cues to others. At the same time, we all practice the skill of reading nonverbal cues. Each day we come into contact with people we do not know. Yet we may quickly make assessments of their personality or their mood simply by noting facial expression or gestures.

Even though we do make use of nonverbal messages with people we scarcely know, the area in which nonverbal communication plays the most important role is in our close, interpersonal relationships. The marital relationship, in particular, provides a situation in which we become very familiar with the moods, gestures, and habits of our spouse. We may be able to read our mate's mood at a glance and may react accordingly.

All of our senses are involved in nonverbal communication—but most particularly the sense of sight. Our eyes pick up countless cues from those around us, and we use those cues to determine how we will react to the people we are involved with each day.

We have all heard of "women's intuition." In fact, studies have shown that women may actually be much better than men in reading and understanding the nonverbal cues given by others. It has also been noted that women tend to concentrate most on the face and eyes, while men pay closer attention to tone of voice and body gestures.

While the ability to "read minds" is probably not an extremely desirable skill, it is helpful to be attuned to the nonverbal cues being given by others.

Six basic emotions have been identified by researchers of human behavior. They are: happiness, sadness, fear, disgust, surprise, and anger. Of these, happiness is felt to be the easiest to read. In addition, these emotions may be intensified, reduced, neutralized, or masked.

We neutralize our emotions when we pretend we have no feelings. When emotions are masked, we substitute one emotion for another in an attempt to conceal our feelings. For instance, many people may keep a smile on their face even though they are angry.

Studies conducted through the use of split-second photography reveal that the range of human expression is changing constantly. Most emotions can be expressed in less than one-fifth of a second, and many are a mixture of the six basic emotions.

In addition to the wide range of human emotions, there are often inconsistencies in verbal and nonverbal communication which may make your task of interpreting these emotions and messages even more difficult. For example:

• You've met your husband for lunch, and as the time approaches 1:00, you ask him if he's in any hurry to get back to the office. As he hurriedly assures you that there's "no rush," you notice that he's stealing frequent glances at his watch.

• You have just received some disturbing news while at an

important business conference. In an effort to maintain your composure, you hide your feelings by assuming a rather shaky smile.

The task of accurately decoding nonverbal messages can be extremely difficult. Following are some suggestions for becoming a more effective reader of nonverbal communication.

• It is very helpful to know the background of the situation. What has just happened? What would your own reaction be? To illustrate this point, consider the typical expression associated with fear. Now consider the expression we commonly associate with surprise. They are so similar that we could easily misread a situation where one of these expressions was given.

• Be able to pick up rapid messages. Emotions are very fleeting. Also keep in mind the range of human expressions and be aware that many emotions are not "pure" but are blends of two or more feelings.

• Always check your perceptions with the person you are attempting to "read." This will avoid misunderstandings that could develop because of inaccurate interpretations.

The understanding of nonverbal cues is an excellent means of increasing your overall communication skills. However, it is important to remember that most people value their privacy. Take this into consideration before you spontaneously remark, "I know what you're thinking!" or "When you wave your hand like that and glance up at the ceiling, I can tell that. . . ."

Use thoughtfulness and tact when dealing with others. There is a fine distinction between imposition and constructive perception. Be attuned to the subtle cues that may aid your communication and thereby improve your relationships, but don't impose on the privacy of others.

Finally, be aware of the type of nonverbal messages you are giving to those around you. Perhaps you've had somebody make a comment like, "Do you ever have an odd look on your face!" Become aware of your expressions and what they mean. Are you accurately presenting a true picture of your feelings, or are you "masking" them behind a facade of false cheerfulness or apathy?

Remember—honesty is a very important aspect of interpersonal communication. If you are not being verbally honest with those around you, you may find that your expressions are giving you away.

The Child Set in Our Midst
by Maxine Hancock

And Jesus called a little child unto him, and set him in the midst. . . Matthew 18:2.

I come from a family of four children. Our Christmases were happy, exuberant affairs. But as we moved into our later teens, Christmas became rather quiet. The old excitement, the irrepressible childish joy in giving, even the overeating to groan point, all were memories from the past. Murmurs of appreciation for exchanged housecoats and fountain pens replaced whoops of delight over new toys. At the table, polite restraint prevailed. My brother and sisters and I, now into high school and college, were growing up. And something seemed to be missing from Christmas.

And then came Afshan's Christmas.

Afshan and her family came into our lives in early fall when her father came to inquire about renting our basement suite. His wife and two children were soon to arrive from Pakistan to join him for his second year of doctoral studies at the university. Just a few evenings later, he brought them home from the

airport and proudly introduced them. His wife—a tiny, exqui-
sitely beautiful young woman, her dark skin accented by slender gold bangles, her slender form gracefully draped in a rich,
deep-red sari. His son—a fat and placid baby. And his daughter
—fine boned and lithe, a little girl with short cropped black hair
and the shy-curious manner of a mountain chipmunk. Half
hiding in the draperies of her mother's sari, Afshan looked back
at us with black eyes that danced with interest and intelligence.
In an instant I loved her. Afshan, not quite six, would form the
living link between the household downstairs and our own. And
it would be she who would bless that year—and that Christmas
—with special memories.

She learned English with the incredible ease and grace of a
child and soon chattered gaily and endlessly at every encounter.
Often in the evenings as I sat at my desk studying, there would
be the quick movement of a little shadow and then two tiny
hands, always cool, would be pressed over my eyes. "Guess
who?" Afshan would cry. Somehow, I always guessed. I would
stop for a few minutes to play a game or tell a story, or we
would sit together at the piano and sing a song together.

It was only natural that we would include the family from
downstairs in our Christmas plans that year. But we could not
have guessed how Afshan would rekindle our Christmas. In the
weeks before the great day, she was a constant interrupter.
Everywhere I was, she wanted to be. She watched as I wrapped
gifts, a tireless interrogator. "Why?" was the question she asked
unflaggingly. About everything. As a child from a Muslim
family, she found everything new, everything exciting. This
was, after all, her very first Christmas.

From the comments of her parents, it soon became evident
that Afshan was also an interpreter. As faithfully as she could,
she repeated to them the Christmas story and the meaning of
the traditions. All her questions culminated on Christmas

evening when her mother turned to me and asked quietly, "Now, please tell me the whole story of Christmas."

The whole story of Christmas. As I tried to tell it, simply and truly in words our guests could understand, the overwhelming wonder of God's love expressed in our Lord Jesus Christ swept over me in a new way.

When at last that special Christmas day was done, we all agreed that the laughter and glee of a little child had transformed our quiet Christmas; her questions had given it a new dimension. Afshan had been the "little child . . . set . . . in the midst," a child who had interrupted us, interrogated us, and who had, unconsciously, interpreted anew to us the whole wonderful Christmas event. Mirrored in her happy face, echoed in the lilt of her laughter, reflected in the wonder in her eyes was the fresh discovery of Christmas. "Unto us a child is born, unto us a son is given" (Isaiah 9:6). For Christmas is about Jesus— God come to us as a child; Jesus—the Child set in our midst. And it is children who help us understand best what that means.

In a world as busy and as selfish as ours, each child is born as an interrupter. Careers are suspended and orderly routines rendered meaningless. Afshan's interruption of my evenings of study was a tiny disruption compared with the interruption I have since experienced with my four children. Not one of them asked, before crying in the night, whether perhaps I might need a whole night's rest. Not one of them asked, before running to me for help during the day, whether perhaps I might be busy at the moment.

The interruption of a child is probably best understood by my friends who have waited several years into their marriages before introducing a child into their well-ordered lives. "After seven years of more or less peaceful adult interchange, our lives are in sudden upheaval," one friend wrote. The birth of their first child had, predictably enough, transformed their tranquil home into parental bedlam.

Those of us who are parents have all known times when we have responded to our children's pressing interruptions with less than real grace. I know that sometimes I was positively peevish about the demands they made. And I remember wondering why the nighttime cry was always, "Mamma!" Did the children think Daddy disappeared after sundown?

Nonetheless, at moments when I was clear-headed enough to actually think about significances, I was aware that each interruption could serve to remind me of the Christ Child who came as the great Interrupter. Every life that intersected his was thrown into an entirely new order—which must have felt like total disorder. Mary, whose village wedding plans were scuttled and whose reputation permanently shadowed. Joseph, who had to surrender the control of a quiet, well-managed life to a God who appeared in angelic visitation and vision. The wise men, whose intellectual star-gazing suddenly precipitated them into action, taking a trek with an unknown destination. The shepherds, whose dull pastoral vigil suddenly exploded with angelic choirs and announcements of cosmic importance. And Herod. Maybe he was the most upset of all, just because he resisted the interruption of the Child born to be King.

The Lord Jesus Christ comes in the same way to each of us. His presence once among us means that we must stop to consider who he is and why he came. And when we do, our lives are wonderfully interrupted. In Jesus, God's claims on our lives are expressed. Each of us must stop to consider what return must be due a God who loved us enough to give us his Son. And life cannot be the same again.

Each child not only interrupts by his presence, his needs, his very existence. He also interrogates. He asks thousands of questions. Afshan, in her pink party dress and wrinkly long brown stockings, beside me as I set the Christmas table asking, "Why do we need two forks? What is this big spoon for? Why do we put the glasses there? Why not here?" Every child asking, asking, asking. For each must form a world view from bits and pieces, many apparently illogical or even terrifying. He must build connectors between those bits by asking questions. And adults must answer, answer, answer.

As we answer the questions of our children, we remember that he asked questions, too. The Christ Child came as a questioner. We have no record of his childhood questioning, but Mary must have needed all the resources she had stored up to ponder in her heart to answer all that he asked. At the age of twelve he was found by his anxious-hearted parents "sitting in the midst of the doctors, both hearing them and asking them questions" (Luke 2:46). However astonishing the questions he put to the learned theologians, they could scarcely have been more pointed than the question he put to Mary and Joseph when they came to claim him: "How is it that you sought me? Did you not know that I must be in my Father's house?"

He would go on asking questions as an adult: infuriating, provoking questions; tenderly probing questions; questions that would leave his hearers breathless in admiration or gnashing their teeth in fury. A fun and fruitful Bible study is to follow the trail of question marks through the Gospels—and really see what he asked. He asked questions that produced the anguish of spiritual self-examination: "Who do you say that I am?" Or that other painful question, put three times to Peter: "Do you love me?" And these are questions he still puts to each of us. They are questions which each must answer, for we cannot ignore or evade his questions. He who comes as the great Interrupter also comes into our lives as the great Interrogator.

But he is more. He is also the great Interpreter.

Afshan, for whom every aspect of Christmas was new and

exciting, made Christmas new to me. As I answered her questions and listened to her reponses, I found the joy and wonder
of the celebration born afresh in my heart, too. Like her, every
child in our homes serves as an interpreter. Children can teach
us, if we will let them, how to see again.

I remember flopping in the shade of a line of trees on our
pasture, hot and tired after a hike and picnic with the children.
One of our girls held a sheet of white paper between us and the
tall pasture grass. Suddenly, we were looking at a black and
white shadow play of intricate lines as the setting sun cast the
shadows of graceful grasses on the screen of paper. As we
watched the infinitely changing beauty of those lines, I realized
that a child had become an interpreter. She had shown me
something I had forgotten how to see, as our children so often
have done.

Far greater, of course, is the message interpreted to us by the
Child who was given, the Son who was born. For the Christ
Child came as Interpreter. "No one has ever seen God," the
Evangelist states; "the only Son . . . has made him known." By
his life, Jesus intepreted to us God's love; by his death, he
interpreted at once God's justice and mercy. In his teaching,
Jesus took the earthly, everyday things and by them interpreted
the kingdom of heaven to us.

To me it is wonderful to reflect on the fact that his work as
Interpreter is still going on. His work for our redemption is
finished, but we read in Scripture that the risen and exalted
Christ "always lives to make intercession" for us. He who came
as a child to interpret God to us is now the exalted Lord,
interpreting us to God!

Each Christmas, I want to capture again some of the wonder
Afshan showed me, some of the awe at the mystery of God-
become-Child. I want to stop to really hear the voices of the
children in my life—interesting in themselves and pointing to

the One who became a child among us. I want to ask myself some questions about how I have responded to the Christ Child. Have I allowed his interruption of my priorities and selfishness? Have I answered his interrogation honestly, crying out from deep within my heart, "You are the Christ . . . and I love you"? Have I worshiped the invisible, immortal God he came to interpret to us, hushed before his holiness?

At this Christmas season, as I gather with other Christians, we will say the family prayer we can say only because of Christmas. I will take a deep breath as I realize again that he who came to us as a child invites me now to come to him as a child. The old words, and the sweet old celebration will be new again as we pray together, "Our Father . . ."

Are You a Workaholic?
by Linda Harris

Harold built his business from the ground up. He learned his trade as a teenager. Soon after he was married, he went into business for himself. A new business takes hard work, and Harold was willing to give it. On the outside, he seemed to be a happy, successful, self-confident person. But Harold had some deep problems hidden inside.

Going to church and being a Christian did not seem to bring much joy to Harold. Church and Christianity were more of a duty to him than a privilege.

Harold's oldest son was a disappointment. Though the son was in his early twenties, he often acted like a child. He dropped out of several schools and colleges and could not keep a steady job. Harold's other three children also seemed to be drifting away from the family.

Harold's deepest hurt concerned his business. He had recently built a new building, costing over a quarter of a million dollars. But business began to drop because competitors with less overhead were able to underbid him. Harold put more and more effort into his work but received less and less satisfaction from it.

All of Harold's problems stemmed from one source—his business meant everything to him. His employees, his family, even God and the church were secondary to his work and his success as a businessman. Harold was a workaholic.

The word *workaholic* is a recent addition to the English language. Derived from the word *alcoholic,* it denotes a person addicted to work, just as an alcoholic is addicted to alcohol. Wayne Oates, the psychologist who coined the word, defines a workaholic as "a person whose need for work has become so excessive that it creates noticeable disturbance or interference with his bodily health, personal happiness, and interpersonal relations, and with his smooth social functioning."

A speaker at a seminar I attended some time ago defined a workaholic as "a person who must work at everything he or she does." And Marilyn Machlowitz, psychologist and author of *Workaholics,* admits to being a workaholic and says a workaholic "is someone who loves and lives to work."

The term *workaholic* means something different to each person. But if we go back to the word from which it was derived—*alcoholic*—we get the picture of something destructive and unhealthy. Marilyn Machlowitz calls her workaholism "a delight, not a disease." She likes to work, but—and this is the key—she likes to do other things, pursuing other interests and getting plenty of exercise.

While true workaholics may seem to have other interests and may get exercise, they often do them compulsively, just like they work. A person who truly likes to work and balances it with other interests and activities is not in the same danger as a true workaholic. An alcoholic does not just like alcohol—he or she is dependent upon it. And this is where the true workaholic is identified—a person who cannot stop working because he or she is emotionally dependent upon it.

If some people who like to work and spend a lot of time at it aren't workaholics, what are they? Better words to describe them might be "devoted," "dedicated," or "consecrated." The work of a workaholic, no matter what it is, controls him, rather than his controlling it. On the other hand, dedicated persons are devoted to their work, but they do not let their work possess them.

To determine whether one is a workaholic or just a dedicated person requires much self-evaluation. The true workaholic may feel it is a waste of time to do so much self-searching. But unless workaholics take time to assess their lives, they may be forced to stop and take a good look at themselves. Many workaholics have found themselves flat on their backs with heart attacks, bleeding ulcers, or other severe health problems. They are the lucky ones, because others die before they identify the problem.

Workaholics often have family difficulties and may find themselves faced with a divorce because a spouse has been ignored too long and needs more attention. Or a son or daughter may get in trouble in order to get their workaholic parent's attention.

To help us decide if we are workaholics, the following questions can be prayerfully and truthfully answered. If we aren't truthful, we are cheating ourselves and our loved ones of the person we could be. There are no right or wrong answers and no scoring system. Only we, with God's guidance, can determine if we are guilty.

• What is my motivation for work? Is it money? prestige? approval? my own satisfaction? belief in a cause? to meet the needs of others?

• Do I worry about money? The truly dedicated person works for the cause, not for the amount of money involved.

• Do I spend time doing other things I enjoy? with my family? relaxing and "doing nothing"? A workaholic may do other things just because it is expected but have a difficult time relaxing and doing nothing.

• Do I quit when I reach my limits? Do I know my limits? If workaholics push themselves too far, their productivity will decrease, but they will go on anyway.

• Do I take care of my body? get enough exercise? get enough sleep? eat regular, nutritious meals? drink too much coffee or soft drinks? Workaholics usually neglect their health. They say they can get by on little sleep, but they drink coffee or colas to stay awake. I once heard a speaker describe the typical workaholic perfectly: "He spent his health to gain his wealth; he spent his wealth to try to regain his health."

• Do I often work through my lunch break or coffee break? work more than fifty hours a week?

• Am I satisfied with my work? or do I always think I could have done better? Workaholics are driven because they are never satisfied with a less than perfect job. A psychology professor was determined not to be a workaholic and encouraged his students in the same way. He said one could get 95 percent results by expending only 5 percent of the energy needed to get 100 percent results. The workaholic is the person who spends the other 95 percent of energy for the extra 5 percent results.

• Do I feel indispensable? What would happen if I became ill and someone had to take my place? Do I know how to say no when asked to take on extra work?

• Do I often talk about my work in social situations? particularly, bragging about how much or how hard I work?

• Do I set goals for myself? Are they realistic and attainable? Do I measure my effectiveness against those goals? Goals are good and all good workers use them. But workaholics tend to set theirs too high and then feel they've failed if they don't attain them. They also tend to measure themselves against another person's accomplishments rather than against reasonable goals. They see someone in the place they want to be and forget how long it took that person to get there.

• Do I have time to spend with God? reading the Bible and praying? If work is first in a person's life, God often gets pushed out. But if God is first, we will always find time to spend alone with him, just enjoying his presence and feeding on his Word.

The Master's Example

Jesus should be our example in all phases of our lives, including this one. If anyone ever felt compelled to work hard, it must have been Jesus. He saw so much that needed to be done, and he knew he had only a few years to do it. His compassion was great, and the needs around him were apparent. At times the crowd demanded so much that he had no time to eat, and his family became concerned for his health (Mark 3:20-21).

But Jesus took time for himself. He spent long hours alone. (See Mark 1:35; 6:46; Luke 6:12.) He spent this time talking with his Father. This, no doubt, included time to think about what had happened, what he was doing, to examine priorities and lift these matters to God in earnest prayer.

In Jesus' life we see a balance that should be present in our own. He worked hard, but he did not overwork to the exclusion of all else. Neither did he feel rushed by urgencies. When Mary and Martha sent word to Jesus that their brother was dying, he did not go immediately. He knew it was more important for him to go later. Jesus' raising Lazarus from the grave was a more astounding miracle than raising him from the sick bed would have been (John 11). Jesus noticed the workaholic tendencies in Martha and advised her to slow down and listen as Mary was doing (Luke 10:38-42).

Following Christ's example may not be easy, especially if

we've been a workaholic for a long time. But with God's help, we *can* change. Here are a few suggestions to get us started.

- **Don't take unfinished work home.** Most things will wait until morning. Efficiency levels can be lowered by constantly taking work home.

- **Make appointments to be with family and keep them.** Make a date to go out with your spouse. Make time to spend with the children, individually as well as together. When these appointments come, really *be* there, mentally as well as physically. Listen to what the family says, not only directly to you, but also to each other; and respond to them in love.

- **Delegate work to others.** Some persons do work that others should do. Let each do his own work. Don't accept any extra work without considering it carefully. Others are competent also.

- **Take sick leave.** When the workaholic realizes he is coming down with a cold or the flu, he will keep working just to prove he won't let a little illness get him down. But we'll actually get more done by taking care of ourselves when we first get sick.

- **Tell the family or a close friend that you want to change and need their help.** Be accountable to them, and talk with them regularly about any progress.

- **Analyze schedules.** Determine how much time can be spent on each activity. Work to better balance the daily schedule.

- **Thank God for everything** (1 Thess. 5:18). Resist the tendency to think that everything one has came by the work of one's own hands.

- **Take time for meditation, Bible study, and prayer.** No other daily activity is as important as this. Take time for Christian fellowship—in church, Bible studies, and social activities.

- **Listen carefully to God.** Seek his will. He has a ministry for each of us. This may or may not be related to our work. As we become involved in a ministry, we may find ourselves working just as hard as we were before. We need to make sure our desire to work is due to dedication and devotion rather than workaholism.

A person can be a workaholic for God as easily as for a secular employer. Overworking for God may seem more acceptable because "it's for a good cause." But remember that a workaholic has an unbalanced life, and if we are neglecting our family, health, or personal time with God, we are not living according to God's plan for our lives.

Elizabeth's return

by Dick Heinlen as told to Norma West

Twelve years ago I was a U.S. Army chaplain (*Cha* in Vietnamese), sharing the pain and death and suffering of my unit and too often feeling impotent to ease that suffering.

The assurance in Romans that "neither death, nor life, nor angels, nor principalities . . . nor powers . . . will be able to separate us from the love of God" took on new meaning when mortar shells were whistling overhead. I was not immune to the same afflictions that I was committed to help ease in others. Sometimes feelings of loneliness—longing for home, my wife, children, family, all that was familiar to me—were almost unbearable. I confess that many times I was so preoccupied with that loneliness and with the fear of being in the combat zone that I was not always in touch with the comfort of my faith.

Consequently, the visits to an orphanage run by Roman Catholic sisters north of Saigon provided moments of sanity amid chaos. In the midst of war, the children gave us a touch of home and kept us human.

We always left the orphanage with a mixture of emotions— gratitude for the change of pace and privilege of going there,

From *The Lutheran,* 7 Mar. 1984. © Copyright 1984 by The Lutheran Church in America, 2900 Queen Lane, Philadelphia, PA 19129. Used by permission.

rage against all wars that brought suffering to little ones, gratitude that our children were safe at home with all their needs met by a loving parent—and an unbearable desire to be home. For me, it was also a realization of obedience to Christ's commandment that we love one another.

Mutual delight existed between children and soldiers. The children would see us coming down the trail and run to the gate, laughing and shouting. The men hid candy in their shirt pockets and the children swarmed each time the truck arrived —except for one little girl with eyes that looked too big for her face, who peeped out from behind a sister's skirts. She captivated me the first time I saw her. I knelt and reached out to touch her and speak to her but, terrified, she retreated further behind the sister. I told her I loved her and asked her to tell me her name.

"She cannot speak, Cha, and she will let no one touch her. We call her Elizabeth but no one knows her real name or how old she may be," the sister said.

They thought her to be 6 or 7 years old. Terror had stilled her voice. She had been found with a group of unrelated villagers who witnessed what had happened and told Elizabeth's story to the sisters. Her family had been tortured by the Viet Cong as she watched. She had seen her father skinned alive and her mother burned alive, and unable to deal with such horror, she retreated into a world of silence, terrified at the sight of a man. No one at the orphanage knew how long she had lived behind that aloof wall of silence.

I visited with all the kids, but Elizabeth became almost a surrogate daughter. I always sought her out to tell her I loved her and spent time especially with her. She kept her distance and never spoke—just looked at me solemnly with those haunted eyes—until one day she left the safest of places and ventured out a little. Yet she remained at a safe distance. Several weeks later we drove up the trail and, as usual, I looked for her. My heart caught in my throat, for she was walking slowly toward the gate to wait for us with the other children. "I love you Elizabeth," I told her and smiled. As expected, she did not respond. She continued meeting us at the gate after that day but always stood a little apart from the others.

I wanted to tell her that I did not want to make demands on her to talk to me—I just wanted to love her. I confess that I did not consciously consider that the liberating love of God, loving her through me, would set her free from that silent world of pain and terror, because I was too preoccupied with how she twisted my heart. Any progress was almost imperceptible. She still would not talk to me or let me touch her. I had to be content with loving her from a distance.

Three weeks before I was transferred, we drove up the trail and saw the children at the gate. As always, I sought out that lone figure that had become so important to me. I sighed, for I did not see her. But there wasn't time to look long because the children were climbing all over us as we sat in the jeep. One child had crawled onto my lap. As I turned, I held my breath. Softly, quietly settling herself back in my arms, as though she had always belonged there, was a little girl with big, dark eyes and long, shiny black hair—Elizabeth! I was afraid to move, afraid she would bolt, but she seemed perfectly at ease. She had never let me touch her in all these weeks, had not spoken for an undetermined length of time.

With great difficulty, I choked out, "Elizabeth, Elizabeth, I love you." She looked up into my face and I saw a little tear form in the corner of one of those big, soft eyes.

"Cha," she whispered. "Cha."

So often we forget that, whether we are conscious of it or not, God uses us every day to work his miracles big or small. Although I left the Saigon area soon after Elizabeth broke silence and let down her wall of fear to creep into my arms, it was my joy to remain there long enough to see her blossom into a more normal child. She began talking freely and relating normally to the other children. She became whole. She had returned.

At times memory of her haunts me and I long to know where she is today, what has happened to her, but those questions will likely remain unanswered in this life.

I owe her so much. She taught me the power of love and caring in a way that was new to me. She taught me that the human spirit can endure untold horrors and triumph in the face of terror with consistent, patient caring. She taught me that the love of God, loving through us, can break the strongest barriers and free a spirit to soar.

To Wake a Meaning
by Bruce Hekman

James Stephens in *The Crock of Gold* writes: "I have learned
. . . that the head does not hear anything until the heart has
listened, and what the heart knows today the head will understand tomorrow."

That is one of the important reasons for Christians to read
good fiction. Good books are an imaginative re-creation of life,
providing the reader with an experience with living, not just a
knowledge about life. Good books help us know our culture and
our humanity by reaching the heart, by recreating the past for
reflection, by creating the future for contemplation, by showing
us the implications of human values, choices, and commit-
ments.

Good books "freeze" human experience, imposing pattern
and structure, providing a beginning, middle, and end to the
joys and sorrows of everyday living in stark contrast to our
own, often chaotic lives and experiences that make it so difficult
for us to think clearly and reflect deeply. Good books give us
an opportunity to savor the richness of our own experiences,
and provide a distance and detachment from our own deepest

fears, struggles, and conflicts so we can think more clearly about them.

The words of the wise, the author of Ecclesiastes tells us, give pleasure to the reader, but also serve as both "goads" and "tent pegs." When a book challenges our assumptions about life, it acts as a "goad" prodding us out of our narrow, provincial world—the "one-dimensional barrenness" decried by Dr. Calvin Seerveld in *Rainbows for the Fallen World.*

The best books always make us just a little uneasy, and a little less certain about our way of thinking about other people (such as migrant workers, Russian peasants, or the old, the impoverished, the rich, the middle/upper/lower class), as well as their cultures and their traditions. Such goading makes us more sensitive to other human beings, an important step towards service. Such goading forces us to test our beliefs and values with the touchstone of the *Bible,* often leading to a confirmation of the truth, but also to new insights.

When good books confirm our experience as humans created in God's image, they become "tent pegs," anchoring us more firmly in the truth. For example, the Narnia Tales of C.S. Lewis, and the imaginative works of Madeleine L'Engle and others, profoundly and beautifully confirm that we live in a world of good and evil; a world that is often a battleground between the forces of darkness and the forces of light; a world in which the power of God is everywhere made manifest, often through the obedient service of very ordinary boys and girls, men and women.

Christians of all ages need to read good fiction, because good books enrich our lives. As Dr. Henry Zylstra wrote in an essay "Why Read Novels?" published in 1956, "by universalizing ourselves in the significant experience of others there is more of us that is Christian—that can be Christian than before."

But so much of what appears in print is second-rate, and the reading of it such a waste of time and money, as well as an assault upon one's sensitivities, that we have despaired of reading fiction ourselves and consequently neglect the importance of nurturing the reading habit in our children and grandchildren. The Christian press is often quick to review and promote "Religious Books" but slow to give their readers help in sorting through the flood of other fiction for readers of all ages. It is a mistake to leave the reviewing of this latter class of books to secular magazines that are too often insensitive to issues that are a part of a Christian's definition of "good" books.

Nevertheless, there are many ways to promote reading of good books, a habit that needs to be learned early in life and nurtured by sensitive Christian adults. Here are some simple, common-sense ways to begin.

Read books aloud! Every child should remember with great tenderness the frequent regular experiences of being read to while snuggled on someone's lap. Such shared experiences and the discussions that often follow can be some of the most significant, memorable learning experiences a child can have. Some families continue the practice until their children are teenagers.

Make time for books! If reading is important, we need to make time for it, and not just vainly hope that somehow we'll find a free minute later on. Many families have discovered reading by banishing the TV set, if not completely, at least from all but a few carefully chosen hours in each week. Others set a time for family reading—an hour before bedtime, or just after supper when everyone gathers in the living room, kitchen, or den to listen to a story, or read silently together. Some schools now set aside a time each day when everyone in the building, from custodian to principal, reads.

Make books available! One of the amazing ways technology has changed our lives is to make printed material easily and inexpensively available to everyone. Public, school, and church libraries bulge with books; bookstores and bookstands are everywhere.

Every child should know the thrill of owning books of his or her very own, in addition to experiencing the pleasure of borrowing books from libraries or sharing books from friends. Christian families in which reading is important will always have books within easy reach of everyone, and a special place to keep them.

Books make wonderful gifts. Librarians and bookstores can give you good advice, and Gladys Hunt's *Honey for a Child's Heart* is a treasure store of good advice to Christian parents looking for good books to make available to their children. If you can't decide what book to select, give a gift-certificate or some cash with a note asking that it be spent on a book. The experience of spending time in a bookstore, selecting a book to buy for yourself is a delicious one, and habit-forming too! With a little gentle guidance from adults, children can learn how to select good books themselves.

Read books yourself! Children do as you do, and say as you say. If you say "Reading is important," but your children seldom or never see you reading or hear you talking about what you're reading, chances are they will also be non-readers who will tell their children about the importance of reading good books.

George Macdonald, 19th century pastor and author of fairytales, wrote in an 1893 preface to the American edition of *The Light Princess,* "Art . . . is there not so much to convey a meaning as to wake a meaning. The best thing you can do for your fellow, next to rousing his conscience, is—not to give him things to think about, but to wake things up that are in him; or say, to make him think things for himself."

Good books touch the heart and nudge the Christian toward the full dimensional obedient life that is our calling.

Gethsemane: A Battle Won . . . A Battle Lost

by Wayne Jacobsen

Gethsemane—a garden, but for this night a battleground as well. For deep within its covering of olive trees the war of the cross was waged. Would Jesus accept His calling to save the world or would He succumb to His distress?

Tormented by sorrow, Jesus called out to His Father. The sobs of His anguish echoed through the trees. But only a stone's throw away His voice went unheard by His three closest friends. The gentle evening breeze had lulled them to sleep.

One of them in particular was hours away from his greatest failure. Gethsemane was his story, too—the story of an opportunity lost. The contrast between these two men, now at the Garden and later through the trial provides an intriguing study on prayer.

The praying Man would rise from His rock and head into the awakening day. His distress was gone. He was confident in the will of the Father. The sleeping one would rise to his challenge only to see his own efforts fail. He would deny the Lord he so deeply loved.

There would be a battle won and a battle lost. In both cases, the outcome was determined hours before in Gethsemane. The victory was not gained in the hour of conflict, but in the time of prayer.

Matthew tells us that Jesus came to the garden sorrowful and troubled (Matt. 18:37). To the three He chose to follow Him further into the garden, He admits His pain, "My soul is overwhelmed with sorrow to the point of death." Then He appeals to them, "Stay here and keep watch with Me."

He goes on a little farther alone and falls in desperation at the feet of His Father. Looking at the nature of His prayer, we can see why it was so effective in disarming His troubled spirit and preparing Him for the cross.

He begins His prayer with honesty. He didn't say what He thought the Father might want to hear, but what He needed to say. "If it is possible, may this cup be taken from Me." His prayers were not spiritualized abstracts but deep cries of heartfelt need, "I don't want to go through with this." How could God deal with His torment if Jesus wouldn't admit He had it?

This was no time for theological niceties. He was at war. The hour of His trial was at hand. He needed God and He needed Him where He hurt. True worshippers will worship in spirit and truth, for they are the kind of worshippers the Father seeks. There is no greater ingredient in prayer than truth. Doesn't that simple trait add depth to the greatest of David's psalms?

Second, He settled His commitment to the will of the Father before He prayed. I'm thankful that His prayer was not an attempt to forego the cross at the expense of our salvation. He was not trying to circumvent the will of God, only asking whether salvation could be accomplished any other way.

Perhaps He thought of the ram that was provided when Abraham offered up his son, Isaac. But it was not to be this time. The Lamb of God was the only sacrifice that could atone for our sinfulness. When Jesus knew it to be so, He still chose to save us regardless of the personal cost. His resolve did not come in gaining His desire, but in submitting to God. "Yet not as I will, but as You will."

How often we make the will of God merely something else to consider along with our other desires. There is no true prayer that does not begin with submission. If you don't start there, God's leading is rarely so appealing that we would choose it of ourselves. Who would ever face the cross if it were just God's suggestion? Jesus' commitment to please God never wavered.

Finally, Jesus looked for His prayer to make a difference. It was not a ritual. He was distressed. If it took three times before the throne to deal with it, then three times He would go.

I love that about Jesus, especially when we hear so much of quick answers to prayers and that unanswered ones are indictments of our faithlessness. Jesus knew the distress that tormented Him, and He knew when it had fled. Persistence bridged the gap between the two.

He was finished when the agony that had brought Him here had fled. He found His refuge in God. Even as His disciples sought to defend Him from His captors, He would quiet them with His secure resolve.

How often do we stop praying before our anxieties, fears or doubts are really dealt with? That wasn't an option for Jesus. He continued to seek God until the presence of the Father set His struggle at rest. When He finished praying, He was ready to meet His challenge. His prayer had been fervent because that's what it demanded to be effective.

Now what of Peter? Obviously, the challenge he faced was not as great as Christ's, nor were the implications of it as great for us. But his struggle that night was nonetheless real.

Note carefully the words of Jesus as He leaves His men in the garden. "Watch and pray so that you will not fall into temptation." Their lack of prayer didn't affect the outcome of Jesus' trial. Though He deeply sought their support, we really can't speculate on how it would have helped Him. But it is noteworthy that He also called them to prayer for their own preparation.

They let their opportunity slip by. Later it would be said of them, "All the disciples deserted Him and fled." Let's look at Peter not as the bad apple, but as the most explicit example of what happened to them all.

Though he had been warned earlier that he would deny his Lord three times by sunrise, it had long since slipped his mind. When he discounted the possibility of denial, he lost his immediate need for the Father.

Now the hour of denial was approaching. Would he stand the temptation? The answer rested not in the strength of his character, but whether he would take the time now in prayer to be filled with God's power and find healing for the fears and doubts that warred for his soul. But as is too often true of us, he couldn't see the battle until the bursts of flame and carnage lay at his feet. Without crises we pray so little and so half-heartedly.

Oh, I'm sure he must have tried to stay awake. I can't envision Peter being so unconcerned about Jesus' obvious sorrow that as soon as He left them Peter turned to the others and said, "Oh, good, let's get some sleep." I'm sure he tried to pray until his eyes got too heavy.

How often do our prayers go only as long as we feel comfortable or until some other fancy strikes us? All the great men and women of God have testified clearly that their most effective prayers always came when they pushed themselves past the point where they wanted to stop.

After finding the three asleep for the third time, Jesus knew it was too late. The opportunity for prayer had passed. Even as

He lamented their sleeping, the flash of torches and murmuring of voices moved closer.

The hour of conflict was at hand. The contrast between Jesus and Peter grows more obvious with each passing moment, and we see how Gethsemane shaped each of their responses.

Peter jumped to his feet, drew his sword and fearfully lashed out at the mob, cutting off the ear of the high priest's servant. A lack of prayer almost always leads to a flurry of worthless human effort! Jesus stood in quiet confidence. "Do you think I cannot call on my Father and He will at once put at my disposal more than twelve legions of angels?" All through His trial and torture He was the epitome of confidence, a far cry from the sorrowful Man who arrived at Gethsemane.

Jesus endured the lies, insults and pain His adversaries heaped on Him without raising voice or hand to free Himself. All Peter could think about by the fire was saving his own neck should they decide to do to Jesus' followers what they were doing to Jesus.

Jesus could already see past His moment of pain. "In the future you will see the Son of Man sitting at the right hand of the Mighty One and coming on the clouds of glory." For the joy set before Him He endured the cross. Peter couldn't see beyond the moment until it was too late and the fruit of his selfishness was bitter weeping.

In the heat of battle, Jesus had proved faithful. He had prepared Himself at the feet of the Father. Peter, forfeiting his opportunity there, endured a night of torture—first with fear and then with failure.

Woe to the army who is serious about the battle only when the enemy is at its threshold. Training, supplies and strategies must be worked out months and years in advance or the battle is lost the moment it begins. Complacency leaves us unprepared for unforeseen challenges.

If we adopted Andrew Murray's perspective, we would quickly become a praying people: "Learn to say of every want and failure and lack of needful grace: I have waited too little upon God, or He would have given me in due season all I needed. And say then too, 'My soul, wait thou only upon God' " (from *Waiting on God*).

Our battles are won or lost in the prayer chamber. When we neglect to carve out effective time with the Father, we go unprepared into our trials or ministry opportunities. Gethsemane teaches us we can do nothing greater than to learn to pray effectively. Learn from Jesus to pray honestly, for God reveals Himself only to the truthful. Pray submittedly, since He doesn't offer His will as mere advice nor His strength to those who won't follow. And pray fervently, until need gives way to His fullness.

The church that rises to power in these last days will be the church that has armed itself in prayer. "Lord, teach us to pray—as much in the absence of conflict as when it abounds—so that we can be your faithful servants."

The Making of a Slowpoke
by Dean Merrill

On March 26, 1983, my actions suddenly became bizarre. My friends wondered about my mental health; strangers found me exasperating, if not un-American. My odd behavior even earned me scowls and threats, stares and head shaking.

On that fateful day, I began to take speed limits literally.

Actually, I was forced into it. I can assure you, I was on no crusade for righteousness or moral purity. As an educated Christian who prided himself on rising above legalism, I disdained the thought of bondage to petty stipulations.

Then came a West Coast business trip. Since my appointments straddled a weekend, I brought my wife along for a second honeymoon. We flew to Portland, Ore., rented a Buick Skylark, and checked into a motel. On Saturday we started a two-day drive to San Francisco.

"Isn't this a joy?" Grace said, relishing the Cascade Mountains as we skimmed down the interstate. Somewhere south of Eugene, Ore., we turned onto a two-lane road to cross the Coast Range and then explore the scenic wonders along the Pacific.

From *Moody Monthly,* Apr. 1984. © Copyright 1984 by Moody Bible Institute, 2101 Howard St., Chicago, IL 60645. Used by permission.

The road was deserted. Once we left a hamlet named Drain, there were hardly any houses on the rugged terrain.

We were cruising down a long incline, practicing a duet for Sunday-morning worship in two weeks (How much more wholesome can you get?), when flashing red lights appeared in my mirror. We weren't alone on this byway after all. How fast had I been driving? Sixty-three, maybe 64?

I pulled to the shoulder and hopped out. Someone once told me you should always go to meet the officer. It shows openness, confidence, and "I-didn't-do-nothing-did-I?" innocence. Besides, you shake out some of the surging adrenaline, and if you're taller than he, you may be able to control the conversation.

"Good morning. May I see your license, please?" He was younger than I was and half a head shorter.

I fished out my Illinois certificate and answered his follow-up questions. "Yes, that is my current address. No, this is a rental car."

"Well, I clocked you doing 70."

I alleged that that was hard to believe, but after all, the rental car speedometer might not be reliable, and besides, those slopes were a bit of a challenge for a flatlander. But I'd be more watchful from then on. . . .

He'd already begun to write.

"Since you're from out of state," he concluded, handing me my citation, "you'll probably want to mail the fine to the address on the back—55 dollars."

And then, with a crack of a smile: "Have a good day."

The mellifluous day suddenly filled with death, the amorous mood turned acrid. I crawled back into the Skylark, restarted the engine, and edged onto the highway. *Eccch!* Grace moved closer, whispering condolences. Her quiet "It's all right, honey" tried vainly to melt my self-condemnation. *Fifty-five dollars!*

This trip was supposed to celebrate our togetherness, and I had torpedoed it all.

A full 20 miles passed before I spoke and then only with long pauses. "Well," I began, "I guess it's time to re-examine my speed-limit philosophy. If this is gonna cost us that much money, I might as well learn something."

Gradually I admitted that my practice up until then had been to drive whatever speed was "safe." Everyone knows the first few miles per hour over the posted limit constitutes the fudge zone, where cops give you the benefit of the doubt. My open-road policy, for example, had been to drive 62 or 63. In a 30 mph zone, 37 was close enough. "Make the best time you can without attracting attention" was my motto.

And it had worked well. I could remember only one other speeding ticket in 24 years of driving. Or were there two?

"Reedsport—8 miles," the sign read—the county seat to which I would involuntarily mail my contribution.

My musing continued, this time along fatherly lines. "Let's switch the topic from speed limits to sex," I said to Grace. "How will I feel if Nathan, when he's 17, decides to adopt my philosophy of not necessarily sticking to the rules, but doing what he can get away with?" I grimaced at the corner I had painted myself into.

Suddenly my mind reverted to when Nathan, around kinder-garten age, figured out the speedometer and its connection to those black and white signs with numbers along the street. Every parent has endured such a stage.

"Daddy, the sign says 40, and you're going 45." I'd wearily answer like every other adult: "Yeah, well, I'm doing all right— you're safe—don't worry." After a month or so, he shut up. Later I endured the whole process again with his younger sisters.

What do I want to say to myself and my kids about complying with laws, both God's and the state's?

Another long pause.

"OK. What would it cost me to take speed limits at face value?" I said.

Grace listened.

"From our house to the airport is 30 miles. If I drove 55 instead of 63 . . ." my mental calculator whirred, "I'd lose three or four minutes." Not as painful as I thought.

The 260-mile trip to my parents' house in Iowa would add maybe an extra half hour on the road. Gradually I ran out of rationalizations. With a needle sitting in the dashboard telling me how fast I was driving and clear signs along the road telling me how fast to drive, I couldn't plead ambiguity. The law said match the needle to the signs. The only remaining question was: Would I obey or rebel?

This was more than minutia. It involved discipleship. God put His finger on a common but substantive part of my behavior. Would I let that too cordial state trooper be, in the words of Romans 13, God's servant to do me good? Or would I in essence tell him, his ticket book, and his statutory code to bug off?

I took a deep breath. "OK. From now on, I shall become the slowest thing on the road," I announced.

Grace laughed. Fortunately for me, the rental car had cruise control. I could make just one decision instead of repeatedly easing up on the accelerator. I punched the button, settled in at 55, and resigned myself to watching a never-ending movie of receding taillights.

However, it was one thing for me to drive 55 mph on a semileisurely trip through the redwoods. It was quite another to drive 30 mph on my way to work Monday morning when I was already running late. My resolve to obedience went through a full-scale trial once back in the urban rat race.

But again, I learned the important lesson that obedience is indivisible. You cannot obey part time and call it good enough. James said this regarding the Ten Commandments (2:10,11). Partial obedience still leaves you a lawbreaker.

I also learned another, less eternal truth about the new digital timepieces that made me so compulsive about individual minutes. In the olden days, when the big hand was a tad to the right of vertical, I called it 8 o'clock. Now, big luminous numerals, 8:03:37, stare at me. I cower in shame at being late and say I should have driven faster. But instead I should have started sooner.

I sealed my fate a few nights later when my children saw the ticket. "Here's what you get when you break the law," I explained, their eyes opening wide with wonder. When I told them what I'd done, and how much it was going to cost, they gasped.

"Do you remember when you first learned to read a speedometer?"

"Yes."

"And you remember how I told you not to worry about a few miles per hour here or there?"

They remembered.

"Well, Daddy has decided that is wrong. I know exactly what the law says and need to do it. So from now on, you have permission to tell me when you notice me driving faster then what the signs say."

They loved the idea. I thought I'd just signed my torture warrant.

But as the weeks and months passed, I discovered that speed-limit driving didn't have to be confining or exasperating. Rather, it was freeing. I no longer calculate what's "safe" in a particular situation or ask myself, "Is this a speed trap? Should I stick to the center lane so I'll go unnoticed?" My mental energies now go toward productive things.

The greatest freedom is not watching for policemen anymore. They can sit behind all the tricky billboards they want. My driving habits bore them, so we ignore one another.

Granted, fellow drivers are not always so placid. Occasionally I feel an urgent soul breathing behind me on a two-lane road. But in a perverse way, I enjoy helping people obey the law. Being salt in the world occasionally means being a good irritant, doesn't it?

I admit I've become strange, and I suppose I'll always be a little out of style. The payoffs are mostly internal. But since that's where I live my life and faith, I'm in a good spot to enjoy them. Besides, for 55 bucks, I think I'm getting my money's worth.

Sorrow's End
by Charles Mylander

Every dramatic answer to prayer mentioned in the Bible came in a time of trouble. Think of the exodus from Egypt, the crossing of the Red Sea, the wall of Jericho. Recall Gideon with his lamps and trumpets before the Midianites, David with his sling before Goliath, Elijah with his prayer of faith before the prophets of Baal. As one's mind races along the track of Bible history—through kings and prophets of Jesus, John, Peter, and Paul—the same truth stands straight and tall: Every crisis gives God a fresh opportunity to use evil for good.

God still answers prayer today in response to human suffering. His arm is not shortened nor his hearing dulled. But in no way do Christians escape the pressures of this world. Do not be misled. Evil is still awful; wrong is still sinful. Pain hurts and suffering brings agony. If the tragedy is severe enough, its memory will evoke only sorrow and tears. (Think, for example, of the holocaust under the Nazi regime.)

But Paul wrote in the fifth chapter of Romans an astonishing thing about trouble: "We also rejoice in our sufferings." The great apostle was talking about far more than laughing at his

From *Eternity,* Mar. 1984. © Copyright 1984 by Evangelical Ministries, 1716 Spruce St., Philadelphia, PA 19103. Used by permission.

troubles. He knew about suffering because he had been there. Whipped, stoned, jailed, run out of town—his hardships numbered more than most people will ever experience. Paul was not alone. Other writers of the Bible affirm that the Christian can expect suffering as part of God's plan for his life. "Many are the afflictions of the righteous," observed David. James assumed his readers would "face trials of many kinds," and Jesus predicted them: "In this world you will have trouble."

My pretty niece Terisue was born with almost no brain. She is six years old but her mental age is closer to six months. My little cousin Richie was only 10 months old when he died of cancer. The malignancy spread with such speed that by the time of his first surgery it was already too late.

I do not pretend to understand why or to second-guess God's reasons. From a human point of view some suffering appears so senseless that only eternity will reveal the secret hand of God at work. The mere thought of the 10,000 hungry people who die each day of malnutrition and related diseases brings a lump to my throat.

The issue we're concerned with here, though, is on a different level. Much depends upon the individual response to the pain that God allows. In tough times every man or woman chooses to become a better person or a worse one. His or her character either matures or crumbles, depending on the response to God while the pressure is on. Most people respond to trials and troubles in one of four general ways.

Four responses

A few people *deny the problem exists.* A bereaved widow tries to live as if her husband were still present, leaving his clothes and personal belongings undisturbed. Years later everything in the house suggests that he may show up at any minute. But her denial will never bring him back or even help her adjust to a new life. In extreme instances, some people live in an imaginary world and wind up in a psychiatric hospital.

A second response is to try to *grin and bear it.* Accepting the tragedy as some kind of fate, these people trudge through life with a weak smile. In Christian garb, these weary saints moan about "bearing the cross," with little evidence of joy or inner peace. The problem with this attitude is that it acts as if God is on vacation; or if he's indeed out there, he does not care enough to help.

In a strange twist of values, some well-meaning people praise the "grin and bear it" pattern as courage. They fail to discern that their unbelief and attempts at self-sufficiency are stumbling blocks which hinder God from acting in their time of need.

A third reaction, all too common, is to *turn bitter.* Resentment eats away at the human spirit like acid on a battery. In times of suffering, these people blame God or another person involved. The tragedy of bitterness is that it ends up self-defeating.

Wise Christians take the fourth approach, something far more helpful. They determine to *yield to the Lord* to make them better people as a result of the suffering. They do not hide from the shock of the pain, but rather endure it like a patient recuperating from surgery. Yielded Christians can count on him to do at least four things.

Four promises

First, *God will give a bounceback that brings seasoned confidence.* Some people seem to never get over trouble. Others with the same kinds of turmoil bounce back a little wiser and more confident for the next struggle. What makes the difference?

The one quality needed is what the Bible calls "perseverance" or "endurance." It is something far deeper than putting up with a nasty situation in one's own strength. The original Greek term that Paul used in Romans 5:3 means sticking-to-it with a brave spirit.

I remember one phone call from a dear friend. On the other end of the line I heard her shocked and heartbroken voice. Her son Kevin worked a night shift on the Air Force base. Early that morning Kevin had come home to find his bride Cheryl lying on their front door step, stabbed to death.

Kevin's childhood training in his Christian home came through in the time of crisis. Some 48 hours after the initial shock, Kevin cried out to the Lord for help.

In the year that followed, Kevin had to learn to live with the aftershocks of the tragedy. As might be expected, he went through many ups and down. He often tried to drown his sorrow in alcohol. Yet by perseverance, both his and that of those who loved him, he whipped the alcohol problem, remarried, and started over in life. Although it was never easy, he bounced back.

Once in a while God causes a person's spiritual growth to jump forward by leaps and bounds. But there is another kind of progress that every Christian must go through. When the Bible uses words like perseverance and endurance it means the inner pain lasts a long time. Developing maturity under stress is more like inching through a minefield during a war than strolling through a flower garden on a summer evening. But God's power enables a man to keep going when all human resources run out. His restoring touch builds a seasoned confidence, not just a temporary bluff based on the feeling of the moment.

Second, through trouble *God purges character qualities and builds the level of maturity.* Persevering when it would seem easier to give up does something wonderful to a man's or woman's inner spirit. God builds a proven character within the person who refuses to falter in discouraging times.

When a refining company buys a load of silver ore and melts it down, the ore takes a lot of heat before the dross separates from the pure metal. In the life of the Christian the Lord at times puts on the heat until everything impure comes to the top. Then he drains off this dross, leaving greater purity underneath. The refiner's goal is sterling silver; God's goal is proven character.

Elizabeth was a godly pastor's wife fighting a losing battle with cancer. In a quiet and unassuming way she had walked with the Lord for many years. Soon after the discovery of cancer her comments revealed the ongoing purging process. "You would think that after all these years I would not face anything new in my Christian life. But I am learning that the Lord always has something new for us, no matter how long we have been Christians."

The impact of Elizabeth's character was amazing. Her funeral was held in the church where she and her husband Clark last served as pastors. The influence of her life, and her level of maturity in suffering brought friends and acquaintances by the hundreds. God had so purged her character that her final testimony moved many of her friends a step closer to the Lord.

Third, *God puts within us the kind of hope that is far more than wishful thinking.* When some people speak of hope it is something like whistling in the dark. But the hope God gives never fades away: it has all the stability of God himself.

It was my privilege to visit Corrie ten Boom many times during the later years of her life. After her first crippling stroke, this strong soldier in the Lord's army could not speak in full sentences nor write, yet she could communicate through single words and hand signals. Only one time did I see the hope of Tante (Aunt) Corrie waver. Doubt about the Lord's nearness had swept over her (not uncommon after a major stroke). Pam Rosewell, her faithful companion, explained to me what Corrie could not fully communicate. As I talked with Corrie, tears coursed down her rough cheeks.

We turned to Matthew 28 and read the promise Jesus made just before ascending to the Father: "I will be with you always, to the very end of the age." Her face brightened as she began to speak with confidence, "always, always, always."

At the time of birth my niece Teri seemed quite normal, except for one eye that strayed. In time her parents began to notice more abnormalities. When the doctors first announced the heartbreaking news to the immediate family, the shock was enormous. However, each one reached for hope in his deepest convictions and found answers grounded in Christ.

"God does not give us anything too hard to bear," her mother Judy commented. She found confidence in the Lord's compassion and grace. Darrell, Teri's father, said, "I believe that the Lord has a purpose in this." In the midst of the pain, he found hope in God's eternal plan.

The skeptic might suspect that such talk amounts to a crutch, that it makes little difference how a person finds comfort since nothing will change the objective facts of suffering and death. The Christian knows that God's kind of hope is also objective, more like a shipwrecked sailor relying on a lifeboat than scraps of driftwood. Something real will happen in the future to change the finality of death, namely the resurrection. Behind the hope stands the powerful God who acts according to his redeeming purposes.

Fourth, *God pours out his own personal love within our hearts.* In Romans 5:3-5 notice the chain reaction that begins with trouble and ends with a heart full of character, hope, and love. The last quality is the most personal. The message is unmistakable. God, in the third person of the Trinity, comes to bind up the bruised and broken. When the pain becomes intense, the Holy Spirit pours God's personal love into the aching heart like a healing salve in an open sore. Ask any pastor if he does not sense God's comforting love at the funeral of a Christian.

Few people have opportunities to attend as many funerals as pastors. In my experience the memorial services of committed Christians and people who didn't know Christ differ dramatically. The difference is not in the music, words of comfort, or content of the service itself. No, the basic distinction is in the underlying tone. A certain feeling of dread permeates the atmosphere of an unbeliever's funeral. Death is either the bitter end or the beginning of an unknown afterlife.

Funerals of committed Christians, however, radiate a feeling of sorrow and love mingled together. The tears are genuine as grief over separation from a loved one takes its toll. Yet the underlying joy slips through. The mourners rejoice that the deceased is with the Lord and feel confident of a future reunion.

Not only at the time of death, but also in the process of dying the Lord is faithful to his own. A Christian is never alone, never without help or hope. God does take care of his children, even when the mystery of prolonged suffering before death has no human explanation.

Tante Corrie wanted to go to heaven and be with Jesus. She spoke of it before her strokes, especially around the time her pacemaker was put in. During one period of grave illness, death seemed close and certain. For over 50 days Corrie ate nothing on her own. She slipped into a coma and no one knew how much, if anything, she could hear or understand. But she made an amazing comeback from that coma and near-death illness. She became alert, ate regularly, and enjoyed guests until the last. I believe God used the closing years of Corrie ten Boom's life as a powerful example and witness to this generation. Far from the false "death with dignity" philosophy, the Lord is teaching the Christian alternative, "dying with love."

Shining through pain

The Bible, if it reveals anything, tells of a God who is adequate in the hour of greatest suffering. He will either deliver his child out of the crisis, give him the strength to endure it, or go with him through the experience to the very end. While no one understands all the reasons for suffering, the Bible does explain some broad principles. The way a Christian suffers serves as a powerful witness to family and friends. The character qualities of patience, maturity, and confidence in God shine out from this person through the pain. Their love for others around them stands in stark contrast to the bitterness expressed by those who reject God's purposes.

It comforts me to recall that the worst suffering of all came to God's own Son. Who can understand the pain of dying on a cross combined with the spiritual suffering of becoming sin for all people? Who can comprehend the sheer agony of separation from God expressed in Jesus' last prayer, "My God, my God, why have You forsaken me?" Yet in the death of Jesus on the cross we see the love of God, who gave his Son to die in our place for our sins.

The follower of the Lord will experience the same trouble the nonbeliever does, but with a difference. The Christian emerges whole because of what Jesus continues to do in his life through the Holy Spirit. He becomes a better person for having gone through the suffering.

100 Years of Compassion
by Chip Ricks

On March 10, 1880, George Scott Railton and seven young women, all dressed in Salvation Army uniforms, marched down the gangplank of the steamship *Australia* in New York City and claimed the country for God.

These eight Christians were not the first to stake a claim in America, but perhaps none were more determined to win souls for Christ and help converts to live victoriously. And, no doubt, the petition of one Christian who bid them farewell in England served to strengthen their determination through the month-long voyage. "Drown 'em on the way, Lord," he prayed, "if they're going to fail You when they get there."

But they did not fail. Last July, more than 11,000 Salvationists from all 50 states gathered in Kansas City to celebrate the Army's 100th anniversary in America. The organization in this country alone now includes 27,000 officers, following a military pattern, who command community centers and outposts in every state, Puerto Rico and the Virgin Islands. Worldwide, the Salvation Army of two million soldiers has established strongholds in 83 countries.

Midway in the 19th century, God gave William Booth, then

Ricks, Chip. "100 Years of Compassion." *Worldwide Challenge,* Jan. 1981, pp. 33-35.

a teenager and a pawnbroker's apprentice, a special compassion for the suffering outcasts of England. Even at his early age, Booth recognized that the gospel meant: 1) caring for the physical needs of every man; 2) cleaning up his self-image to preserve his dignity; 3) leading him to Jesus Christ. In other words, "soup, soap and salvation."

But in 1846 the Nottingham Methodists on Broad Street did not go along with Booth's plan of reaching the alcoholics, the prostitutes, the drug addicts and the poverty-stricken of the slum area called "The Bottoms," only a few blocks from their comfortable Wesleyan Chapel. One Sunday Booth rounded up a platoon of the dregs of Nottingham's slums and, marching them proudly down the aisle, seated them in the "best people's" pews. The outraged congregation ordered him to conceal his "unfortunates" at the back of the church—should there be any further visits.

Although Booth failed to awaken the established church to the needs of those God had placed upon his heart, he could not forget them. Eventually he was ordained a Methodist minister, but he focused on the tenements and alleys of London, a city of three million people, one-third of whom lived in poverty.

On June 16, 1855, this lanky soldier for Christ married Catherine Mumford, who shared his vision of reaching the unloved and unchurched in East London. Just a few years later, Booth resigned from the Methodist Church and took his family into the midst of his mission field.

While raising eight children in near-poverty conditions, the Booths both preached in tents, dance halls, pubs and vacant buildings. In 1867 Booth joined a small group called the Christian Mission and, four years later, became its director. By this time, the mission was holding 140 services a week at 14 preaching stations and feeding hundreds of people daily in soup kitchens. From the Christian Mission came the official organization of the Salvation Army in 1878.

George Scott Railton, who two years later was to lead seven women to America, and young Bramwell Booth, William and Catherine's son, were key figures in setting up the organization. In 1879 William Fry and his three sons brought their musical instruments to a street meeting to accompany the singing. This was the beginning of the Salvation Army band. As the Army spread throughout England, local bands were organized at every post. And Booth's soldiers, whom he referred to as "godly go-ahead dare-devils," were establishing new posts at the rate of three every six months.

But in England and in America, persecution was severe. Salvationists were opposed by saloon keepers, factory owners, tenement owners, government officials and often the established church. In Exeter, England, in 1884, for example, hundreds of Salvationists went to prison for disobeying orders not to preach on the streets.

In the years that followed, this Christian army invaded countries all over the world, winning battle after battle fought for the bodies and souls of men, women and children. Those of us in America know well their "doughnut girl" of World War I, their familiar uniforms operating USO's for servicemen in World War II, their coffee and doughnut stations in disaster areas, emergency relief wagons, clothing stores, Christmas kettles and brass bands.

Perhaps less known are their adult rehabilitation centers for alcoholics, maternity homes for unwed mothers, prison-gate homes for men and women on parole, homes for the handicapped—only a few of their many outreaches.

This past year in the United States, Salvation Army soldiers cared for 55,172 persons in counseling, work therapy and psychiatric aid programs, assisted 7,931 unwed mothers, admitted

23,315 patients to their three general hospitals and provided outpatient care for 80,476 others. More than 74,000 children, mothers and senior citizens enjoyed 55 Salvation Army summer camps, and more than 900,000 days' care was given to children who could not be cared for in their homes. These figures are even more astounding when we remember that the majority of those helped by the Salvation Army are unable to pay for such services.

How are the costs of such extensive programs met? Support comes in a variety of ways. Army trucks collect used clothing, furniture, farm produce, animals—any usable item. What isn't needed is sold for cash. Interested individuals who want to have a part in caring for others give money directly to the Salvation Army. Some programs, like the day-care centers, receive minimal financial aid from the federal government.

But by far the greatest asset of the Salvation Army is its soldiers, dedicated Christians whose primary purpose in life is to win others for Jesus Christ. Much of the budget is raised by their own self-denial efforts. Those working in secular full-time jobs are committed to withholding for themselves only what is needed. Their service to the Army programs is voluntary, without pay. The more than 45,000 bandsmen even provide their own uniforms.

While an officer is provided furnished living quarters, a car and an allowance to raise his family, little is left for luxuries. However, 40% of the officers are from Salvation Army families, well trained in the Army way of life. One officer said, "I never had to ask how a Christian should live. I just watched my parents in action."

Salvation Army officers, all ordained ministers, are under strict Army discipline. They must get permission to marry and cannot marry outside the Army. Wives automatically assume their husbands' ranks and are given assigned duties. Relocation orders generally arrive three weeks before moving date. Families are aware that they are in the service of the King and must be ready to go where they are needed the most.

This willingness to serve all mankind regardless of race, creed or color has pervaded the Salvation Army during these past 100 years. Once an Army captain watching British soldiers being divided according to their churches shouted, "All you chaps who belong to nobody follow me!"

This appeal is true today. The poor, the hungry, the destitute, the unloved people who need to know Jesus—all are the concern of the Salvation Army, ministering in His name, meeting needs with "soup, soap and salvation."

The Lights of Hanukkah Shine on Christmas

by Chip Ricks

Light from thousands of candles will be seen this month through the windows of both Jewish and Christian homes around the world. For those celebrating Hanukkah, the lights will stand as a reminder of a time in Jewish history when the temple in Jerusalem was restored for worship of God, and the seven lamps of the Menorah once again shone brightly. For those celebrating Christmas, the lights will announce to the world the birth of one who declared, "I am the light of the world."

The Jewish celebration is too often ignored by Christians—perhaps because we know so little about it. Yet, Jesus celebrated the festival and called our attention to it by His teaching. The lights of Hanukkah can have deep significance for those of us who observe the birth of Christ.

Hanukkah is the one Jewish holy day not rooted in biblical narrative. The story of its origin is found in the apocryphal book 1 Maccabees. The century following the death of Alexander the Great, Judah was caught in conflicts between Syria and Egypt. During a period of Syrian rule, Antiochus Epiphanes, in an effort to unite his kingdom, decreed that everyone

Ricks, Chip. "The Lights of Hanukkah Shine on Christmas." *Worldwide Challenge,* Dec. 1981, pp. 5-6.

must worship his Greek gods. When the Jews refused to bow before Zeus, the king ordered them to sacrifice hogs and unclean cattle on sacred altars, to leave their sons uncircumcised and to defile themselves with unclean, profane practices.

A huge statue of Zeus was placed in the temple at Jerusalem, and swine were sacrificed on the altar of God. Pagan troops dared to enter the Holy of Holies. They erected altars to Greek gods in towns throughout Judah. Books of the law were burned, and Jews found in possession of Holy Scripture were put to death.

When one of the king's officers entered the town of Modin, he tried to force the priest, Mattathias, to offer a sacrifice to Zeus. In a loud voice the aged Jew answered, "If all the heathen in the king's dominions listen to him and forsake each of them the religion of his forefathers, and choose to follow his commands instead, yet I and my sons and my brothers will live in accordance with the agreement of our forefathers. God forbid that we should abandon the Law and the ordinances. We will not listen to the message of the king, or depart from our religion to the right hand or to the left."

When a weaker Jew obeyed the officer, Mattathias, in a rush of anger, killed them both. Then he fled to the mountains where with his five sons he led a rebellion against Syria until his death. Later, his son, Judas Maccabaeus, marched victoriously into Jerusalem and with his men rebuilt the altar, sanctuary and entire interior of the temple. They made new holy dishes, recovered the incense for the altar, and brought in the table for the shewbread. The beautiful Menorah, the lampstand of pure gold with seven lamps molded together without a seam, was returned to its proper place.

On the 25th day of Chislev, 165 B.C., exactly three years from the day Antiochus Epiphanes had desecrated the temple, the Menorah was lighted and the eight-day purification ceremonies began. But to their dismay, the priests discovered they had only one small flask of holy oil—enough to burn for one night. Legend says, however, that the oil burned continuously for eight days and nights. Like the descent of fire from heaven upon the altar of Solomon's temple, so the miracle of the lighted Menorah was God's confirmation of the cleansing of the temple.

Judas and the congregation decreed that the festival commemorating the event would be observed every year on the 25th day of the Jewish month of Chislev.

Whether or not the legend of the replenished oil is true, the Menorah is an important part of Hanukkah, also known as Festival of Lights or Feast of Dedication, and significant for us as Christians.

We are told about this lampstand of pure gold in Exodus 25:31-40. Here God gave Moses detailed instructions for making it. When completed, the central shaft of the candlestick stood higher than the six branches. The artwork on each of the seven lamps consisted of the three stages of the almond—the bud, the flower and the ripened fruit. The central shaft had four complete sets of these three stages, while the six branches had three sets each.

The 12 symbols on the central shaft perhaps represent the 12 tribes of Israel and later the 12 apostles. The nine symbols on the left branches and the right branches can point to the fruit of the Spirit listed by Paul in Galatians 5:22,23. Certainly we know that God has always intended that His people should bear fruit as they remain close to His light.

Judson Cornwall in his book *Let Us Draw Near* suggests that the lampstand is a symbol of the coming Messiah. Seven, the number of perfection, points us to our God of light. Light has three primary colors; our God is a trinity. While light going through a prism breaks into seven colors, all seven blended together give us white light—God's perfect light.

In a vision that the prophet Isaiah saw, he reported, "The people who walk in darkness will see a great light; those who live in a dark land, the light will shine on them."

Because the Menorah was not to be duplicated for use outside the temple, those celebrating the Festival of Lights in the first century A.D. burned various numbers of lights in their windows or before the doors of their homes. Some chose to light one lamp for each member of the family, some one lamp for each day of the festival—either in ascending or descending order. Not until the fourth century did the special Hanukkah Menorah as we know it today with its eight branches, representing the eight days of purification, and a central shaft to hold the servant candle come into being.

On the night when Jesus was born, surely no light shone brighter than the star of Bethlehem to celebrate the dedication of a temple not made of stone. Later, John the Baptist came announcing Him whose birthday we celebrate during the Festival of Lights. John declared that Jesus Christ was the "true light which, coming into the world, enlightens every man." Jesus did not deny this. "I am the light of the world," he said. "He who follows Me shall not walk in the darkness, but shall have the light of life."

Many who were blind received their sight at the touch of Jesus' hand. But one man in particular was chosen of God to illustrate Jesus' power to bring light to darkness. This happened in Jerusalem just prior to the Festival of Lights. Jesus said, "We must work the works of Him who sent Me, as long as it is day; night is coming, when no man can work. While I am in the world, I am the light of the world." Then Jesus anointed the eyes of the blind man with clay and he received his sight.

But bringing light to the man's understanding was even more

important to Jesus. Note the conversation that took place next: Jesus asked, "Do you believe in the Son of Man?"

The man must have been puzzled.

"Who is He, Lord, that I may believe in Him?"

"You have both seen Him, and He is the one who is talking with you," Jesus answered.

"Lord, I believe," the man replied, and he worshiped Him.

True, Jesus was concerned about the cleansing of the temple in Jerusalem. He went to the Jewish celebration of the Festival of Lights. But on the occasion when He drove the money changers, sheep and oxen from the courtyard, John tells us, Jesus pointed the thinking of the astonished observers to the greater temple—His body. "Destroy this temple," he said, "and in three days I will raise it up."

And so He did. The body of Christ, made up of all true believers, is His cleansed holy temple. Paul wrote, "Do you not know that your body is a temple of the Holy Spirit who is in you?"

The lights of Hanukkah, then, have meaning to us as Christians. When we see the eight-branched Hanukkah lampstand, we can be thankful for the example of a group of courageous people who refused to bow to foreign gods and rejoiced when once again light came to a cleansed temple.

When we see the seven-branched Menorah, we can remember that God's perfect light has been shining down through the ages and that it foreshadowed the birth of our Savior who came to bring men "out of darkness into His marvelous light." This should bring added joy to our Christmas celebration.

The eight-day Hanukkah celebration begins this year on December 21. Like our Jewish friends, let us put our candles in the windows of our homes. In this way we will announce to the world that in our homes and in our lives "the darkness is passing away, and the true light is already shining."

Family Meetings
by Ann Thompson

Want to decrease the conflict and increase the pleasure of your family's daily living? That's what family meetings are doing for us, and they can do the same for you.

Before we started having regular weekly family meetings, discipline was handed down from parent to child. Although my husband Bill and I recognized that this was an authoritarian approach, we used it because we knew of no other way. Like our own parents before us, we disciplined lovingly, but for us the method was not working too well. We faced either rebellion, defiant compliance with the rules, or attempts to ignore the rules.

Not only were we making all the rules for behavior, we were also planning all the pleasant things, such as birthday parties and outings. For example, Bill and I would decide that we were going out to dinner, or to a movie, and then tell the children we were going. Usually they would be pleased or excited, but sometimes we would note that they were less than completely enthusiastic over what we were "doing for them."

So we began to look for a way to improve our relationship

with our girls. In the course of this attempt, we took a parenting class through our local community education program. Through this parenting class we learned different, more creative ways to approach discipline. We discovered that methods of discipline must change as time progresses; what seemed to work well for our parents is not always applicable in a more democratic age. We learned in this class that one of the most effective means of dealing with problems was to have a regular weekly family meeting.

The family meeting is a type of forum for discussing both the joys and problems that confront a family. In a family meeting recently, for example, we accomplished several things. First of all, we opened and closed with prayer, thanking God for each family member and asking for his guidance during the meeting. Then we (1) paid allowances; (2) discussed upcoming dates and events of importance; (3) talked about excessive TV watching and placed a time limit on the amount viewed each day; (4) expressed gratitude for the children's getting off to school easily each morning; (5) talked about good things, such as a recent visit to the state fair, a grandmother's visit, Mary Ruth's good record in the bent-arm hang at school, and Carol's seeing her art teacher at school; (6) planned an outing; (7) talked about how to keep Carol's room neat; (8) set up a schedule of housekeeping chores for each family member; (9) agreed to knock on Carol's door, even if it was open; (10) planned a family restaurant night; and (11) discussed gum chewing—no popping!

All this was accomplished in a one-hour meeting with no arguments, no lost tempers, no hurt feelings. Our life in general, as well as our sense of family unity, has improved greatly since the start of our family meetings.

Family meetings are easy to do. Setting one up is relatively simple, although there are a few basic rules to remember. One person needs to be in charge of the meeting, while someone else keeps the records and accounts for finances. Plan to rotate the officers in a regular order; even a younger child can serve as chairperson with a little help, although older members of the family may need to take the positions of secretary and treasurer.

Set up a regular time for the meeting, and keep it with the faithfulness of a doctor's appointment. If it becomes necessary to change the time or day, be sure that you do so only with the agreement of all members of the family.

Limit your time to one hour, or maybe even thirty minutes at the beginning. A well-planned agenda is the secret of accomplishing a great deal of business in a relatively short time. The chairperson should adhere to the suggested agenda, which should be set out in plain view from one meeting to the next so that family members may place an item on it for the following week's meeting. That way nothing is forgotten when the time for the meeting arrives, although we go over the agenda and make last-minute additions at the beginning of the meeting.

A parent's attitude needs to be courteous, fair, and pleasant. When discussing problems, present them as a personal problem and ask for suggestions about dealing with them. Be willing to hear more than one possible way to solve a problem. Refrain from presenting your own ready-made solution and listen respectfully to all suggestions.

One of the most effective methods for obtaining creative suggestions is brainstorming. Ask all members to suggest possible solutions, no matter how far out the suggestions might seem. Let one member record the suggestions as they come, and when there are no more, offer them to the group for consideration. With a little luck, there will be a solution that satisfies everyone, or at least a workable compromise will be offered.

Often you will be surprised at the number of creative solutions that will be offered. Being asked to help solve the problem fosters a sense of cooperation, as well as a feeling of helpfulness, among all family members.

Listen with as much attention to the problems your children bring up as you want them to give to yours. You need to search each time for a solution that is agreeable to all parties involved.

One of the things that will really make the family meeting something to look forward to is planning for something special. There's no need to plan something special every week, however. We spent several weeks, for example, planning to go to an amusement theme park, and each one contributed each week to a fund for the purpose. The special event does not have to be expensive, either; it could be plans for a family night at home or an outing to the park.

Children and parents alike enjoy making plans for pleasant occasions; the anticipation is half the fun. Furthermore, when all members of the family have input into the plans, they are not only more excited about the event, but more cooperative in carrying out the plans for it. In effect, they feel a sense of responsibility for its success because they participated in planning it.

Decisions reached at the family meetings should not be permanently binding. For one thing, if family members feel that the decision will be in effect forever, they will be less likely to try something new or different. If, however, the decision will be in effect only until the next weekly family meeting, members are willing to experiment with a different, perhaps more creative, solution to the problems presented. Satisfactory solutions reached at family meetings may become permanent at some point in time, although it is understood that anyone may bring up the subject for consideration at future family meetings.

Written minutes are important to help everyone understand and remember what was decided at the family meeting. They should be placed where they can be easily referred to, if necessary. Also, one of the first items on the agenda should be the reading of the minutes and the evaluation of the preceding meeting's decisions.

Although family meetings are as different as the families that take part in them, some basic elements should be present in all of them.

For example, the family meeting needs to be a pleasant experience. There should be a regular time set aside in which good things are mentioned and planning of pleasant experiences is done.

When problems are brought up, remember you are looking for a solution that will be workable for all members of the family. Whereas brainstorming is a valuable technique, offering a simple, pat solution is frequently self-defeating.

Family meetings are not a way for parents to take control of the family. Rather, they are a way of dispersing control and responsibility, a way of letting everyone show caring concern for the others' needs. During the course of a family meeting, family members need to work at being helpful and cooperative with one another rather than competing for attention or control.

Most of all, as you think about beginning family meetings, remember that God's guidance is an essential component for success.

Christian Living in a Non-Christian World
by Albert L. Truesdale

Christians in our day will either present a clear Christian counter to neopagan values or we will be neutralized and eventually consumed by them.

The Christian faith was born into a world marked by religious and moral pluralism; there were numerous competing religions and diverse estimates of right and wrong. Religious options ranged from the ancient Greek and Roman gods whose popularity was waning, to the highly attractive mystery religions that invited their communicants to participate in secret rituals and baptism in the blood of sacrificial animals. In addition to these, the cultic prostitutes of Aphrodite, many local deities, and worship of heavenly bodies invited adherents.

In the Roman empire, human life was often cheapened by various forms of public sport and entertainment, slavery, and infanticide (leaving undesirable infants to die on the hillsides).

Into this kaleidoscope came the Christians, initially viewed by many as just more clutter on the confusing first-century religious landscape. They would, it was assumed, fade into the

From *Herald of Holiness,* 29 Jan. 1984. © Copyright 1984 by Herald of Holiness, 6401 The Paseo, Kansas City, MO 64131. Used by permission.

scenery to become but one more option in the religious super-market. Eventually they would be worn away by the tides of social and political change.

But this did not happen. Eventually, Christianity became the dominant religion of the Roman Empire and went on to provide the foundations for Western civilization. Why did this happen? The reasons are too numerous to list here. But one very impor-tant reason was that the early Christians displayed a set of values that provided a clearcut challenge and option to the pagan moralities. Through their Christ—through His teach-ings, death, resurrection, and meaning—a new vision of human existence was infused into the human stream and Christians were its carriers. Christians were remarkable for their uncom-promising dependence on the New Life that had appeared in Christ, and for their determination to embody that life in a parallel ethic. Those who tried to separate the two were denied the name "Christian."

Leaders such as the apostles Paul, James, and Peter, as well as Early Church fathers such as Clement of Rome and Polycarp of Smyrna, taught the early Christians that genuine faith in Christ had to be demonstrated in a complete reordering of one's existence in the world.

Such a commitment met with ridicule and hostility. Celsus, a learned pagan opponent of the Christians, and many Jewish leaders were scandalized by the Christian movement's "open-ness to people of all races and classes, to women as well as slaves—its concern for the downtrodden, the outcast, the sin-ners" (Georg Forrell, *History of Christian Ethics,* 1:29). Refusal to serve in the military submitted Christians to unending con-tempt. Their commitment to honesty made them appear hope-lessly naive in a rough-and-tumble world. Their refusal to either observe or participate in sports that demeaned the human spirit earned them social ostracism.

But they persisted in their vision. And their vision of what life can and ought to be appealed to increasing numbers of people searching for a life that could provide escape from the sea of pagan death.

A similar challenge faces the church today. Our world is experiencing re-paganization. Traditional moral values, derived largely from the Judeo-Christian tradition, which have to a large extent undergirded Western civilization, are now being replaced by values that draw their inspiration from either atheism, the basest forms of materialism, servitude to astrological bodies, scientism, syncretistic cults, or humanistic self-help programs. Appropriately, a recent book is entitled *Drawing Down the Moon; Witches, Druids, Goddess-Worshipers and Other Pagans in America Today.* This book charts what Theodore Roszak calls "neopaganism."

The diversity of religious and moral options begins to remind us of the first century into which the Christians came.

There is a real danger that we 20th-century Christians will be so much a part of this climate that our values will be too little Christian and too much pagan, and that we will fail as witnesses to the radicality of the gospel of Christ and to the standard of holy living to which the Body of Christ is called.

Nothing is more urgent than that Christian leaders, pastors, college professors, and parents—all of us—ask and live out the answer to the question, "What does it mean to live a distinctively Christian life in a neopagan world?"

There are some fundamental principles that can guide us.

1. Within the Christian faith, people are considered valuable because of their inalienable relationship to God, that is, they are created in His image and are the fundamental objects of His redeeming love.

Hence, it is essentially unchristian to value a person on the basis of such incidentals as sex, nationality, age, race, or social status.

Furthermore, it is essentially unchristian to value institutions —political, economic, religious—above people. Whenever this error is committed, the door opens to all sorts of abuses such as the Nazi Holocaust, racism and sexism, and the shameful drug and sex industries of the industrialized West.

To be truly Christian includes a commitment to justice as the right of each person to lead a fully human life.

2. The kingdom of God and it's righteousness insists that the highest values are those that promote love between people, that refine the human spirit, that utilize this world's resources to improve the common lot of people everywhere, and that generate worship of God as the Father of light and life.

Hence the Christian faith stand unalterably opposed to all forms of materialism, because materialism reduces *the valuable* to physical possessions, to money, and social influence. Today the Christian faith is in danger of being swallowed up by the baals of consumerism even as ancient Israel was swallowed up by the baals of cultic prostitution. Even the beauty of holiness is in danger of being swept aside by such materialistic status symbols as the cost of our carpets, the glamour of our vacations, the brand of our clothing, and the models of our automobiles. If these become the measure of life, then we *must* relinquish all identity with the lowly Galilean who preached the Beatitudes.

Let there come among us a rebirth of Christian values that will point a way out of the endless and enslaving cycles of consumerism.

3. Essential to the Christian faith is an estimate of human sexuality that insists on its fundamentally sacred character.

The Christian faith believes that when human sexuality is cut off from its religious significance, it becomes a degrading rather than an enobling influence. Divorced from its larger context, it produces exploitation of one person by another and a general depreciation of the other values without which human sexuality loses its importance. Viewed as a source of entertainment, it breaks the bonds of covenant and respect that it is meant to symbolize. The cheapening of life in our day is largely the fault of the way our culture profanes human sexuality.

4. Because the New Testament insists that the whole of life should be discipled by Christ, all forms of entertainment and use of leisure time should aim toward refining the human spirit, and not toward a mere gratification of wants.

5. Money and property must be viewed as a means for increased service to humankind and not as an end in itself or as the measure of a person's worth.

To hoard money and to confess faith in God are mutually exclusive ways of life. Jesus put it simply, "You cannot serve God and mammon." We Christians are bombarded with the subtle lie that if we serve God we will prosper financially. We must be wise enough to see that this is but another way of saying that we serve God in order to profit monetarily. This is profanity.

Finally, as Christians, our entire mode of conduct should prepare us to live redemptively among our fellow employees, associates, families, and neighbors. As the Book of James so clearly states, a profession of faith in Christ must legitimate itself in an ethic consistent with what God has said about himself and His world in Christ.

God of the Galaxies, Lord of the Leptons
by Terry Valley

As you read this, you and I are speeding through space at 600,000 miles an hour. That's because Earth is being slung around the center of our galaxy that fast. Yet, even at this fantastic speed, it will take us 200 million years to make one orbit.

Science gives us these facts. Because of that, our view of the universe is widened considerably. We see that we're only a small part of a much greater whole. But that widening of vision goes much farther. We know that our galaxy, the Milky Way, is spread out across space to accommodate its 100 billion stars. Even if we traveled as fast as anything can travel—186,000 miles per second, the speed of light—it would take us 100,000 *years* to cross it.

That's big. But there's more. Science tells us that there are more collections of billions of stars, called galaxies, out there. Moving at maximum speed, 186,000 miles per second, it would take about a million years to go from one galaxy to the next. Since there are about 100 billion galaxies, it would take 100

From *Light and Life,* Feb. 1984. © Copyright 1984 by Free Methodist Publishing House, 999 College Ave., Winona Lake, IN 46590. Used by permission.

billion of those million-year-long trips before we ran out of places to go.

How big does the universe look now? To simply say that it's big is like Noah saying, "It looks like rain."

We are dwarfed to insignificance by the gigantic cosmos surrounding us. Science has opened our eyes to the enormous size of the universe, but it gives no consolation for the insignificance it has forced upon us. If the purpose of science is, as some say, to increase knowledge, then it is an empty purpose, even a sorrowful one. "For in much wisdom is much vexation, and he who increases knowledge increases sorrow" (Ecclesiastes 1:18, RSV).

It doesn't have to be that way. True, looking up at the stars can make us feel small and insignificant. Maybe that's one reason they are there—to keep us humble before our Maker. But if we know something about them, it can comfort us and draw us closer to God. That's where science comes in.

Science informs us that stars are made of atoms. Atoms are tiny. A billion trillion of them could fit into the period at the end of this sentence. Yet, from these invisible pygmies, the largest objects in the universe—galaxies—are made. Galaxies are composed of billions of stars, which are composed of trillions of atoms.

Electrons are members of the lepton family of subatomic particles. They orbit the center of an atom something like stars orbit their galactic centers. But while it may take millions of years for a star to complete a single orbit, the electron makes a billion orbits in a millionth of a second. Think of it: all those electrons in all those atoms, in all those stars, in all those galaxies, making billions of trips around their atomic centers *every second!* And they have done it since the moment of Creation, and continue to do it as you read this. Billions of orbits in billions of atoms in billions of stars in billions of galaxies. . . .

It all gets to be too much, doesn't it? We can't comprehend it. That must have been David's reaction as he lay on his back at night, as a shepherd, looking up at the stars. He didn't have science to tell him about atoms and stars and galaxies, yet he still was overwhelmed by the majesty and scope of it all. In Psalm 139:6, he freely admits, "Such knowledge is too wonderful for me; it is high, I cannot attain it" (RSV).

Isn't that our response, too? We not only have the outward experience of seeing the heavens as he did, but we experience the inner confrontation of knowing how utterly complex and vast is the system that supports those stars. We fail completely to understand how something so astonishingly complex as the universe could not only come into existence but run as smoothly as it does. We simply cannot understand. So we stand in awe, and like David, praise the One who created it.

Psalm 8 begins and ends with praise to God for His creation. But it also contains that feeling of insignificance: "What is man, that thou art mindful of him?" (Psalm 8:4). Looking up at the stars, David felt dwarfed by the vastness of creation and its Creator. Why should God pay any attention to man?

But He does. Not only does He pay attention to us, He gives us brains and the means (science) to use those brains to explore the universe. "Thou hast given him dominion over the works of thy hands; thou hast put all things under his feet" (Psalm 8:6, RSV). Science extends that dominion, but it also has the capacity to deepen our awareness of how much God loves us—if we will only let it.

Jesus spoke of God knowing when every sparrow falls to the ground, of knowing even the number of hairs on a person's head. When I look up at the stars, I know that they are made of atoms, and each atom has electrons racing around it billions of times each second. God is aware of each orbit.

I also know that similar lepton particles are making similar orbits in the atoms of my own body. And God is aware of those, too. From deepest space, the farthest reaches of the cosmos, to the deepest, innermost recesses of my body, God is there. "Am I a God at hand, says the Lord, and not a God afar off? Can a man hide himself in secret places so that I cannot see him? says the Lord. Do I not fill heaven and earth? says the Lord" (Jeremiah 23:23-24, RSV).

And so I am comforted. Though the stars make me feel small, they also remind me that God knows me. He cares. He loves me and takes care of me as intimately as He does the distant stars. Like David, I stand in awe. But, if possible, that awe is even deeper for me. For through science, I see more than just stars. I see the God of the galaxies, the Lord of the leptons.

The Making of a Minister
by Walter Wangerin, Jr.

I wish to memorialize Arthur Forte, dead the second year of my ministry, poor before he died, unkempt, obscene, sardonic, arrogant, old, old, lonely, black, and bitter—but one whose soul has never ceased to teach me. From Arthur, from the things this man demanded of me, and from my restless probing of that experience, I grow. This is absolutely true. My pastoral hands are tenderized. My perceptions into age and pain are daily sharpened. My humility is kept soft, unhardened. And by old, dead Arthur I remember the profounder meaning of my title, minister.

It is certainly time now, to memorialize teachers, those undegreed, unasked, ungentle, unforgettable. In memoriam then: Arthur Forte.

Arthur lived in a shotgun house, so-called because it was three rooms in a dead straight line, built narrowly on half a city lot.

More properly, Arthur lived in the front room of his house. Or rather, to speak the cold, disturbing truth, Arthur lived in a rotting stuffed chair in that room, from which he seldom stirred the last year of his life.

No one mourned his absence from church. The man had a walk and a manner like a toad, a high-backed slouch, and a burping contempt for his fellow parishioners. Arthur's mind, though uneducated, was excellent. He had written poetry in his day, both serious and sly, but now he used words to shiv Christians in their pews. No one felt moved to visit him when he became housebound.

Except me. I was the pastor, so sweetly young and dutiful. It was my job. And Arthur had phoned to remind me of that.

But to visit Arthur was grimly sacrifical.

After several months of chair sitting, both Arthur and his room were filthy. I do not exaggerate: roaches flowed from my step like puddles stomped in; they dropped casually from the walls. I stood very still. The TV flickered constantly. There were newspapers strewn all over the floor. There lay a damp film on every solid object in the room, from which arose a close, moldy odor as though it were alive. But the dampness was a blessing, because Arthur smoked.

He had a bottom lip like a shelf. Upon that shelf he placed lit cigarettes, and then he did not remove them until they had burned quite down, at which moment he blew them toward the television set. Burning, they hit the newspapers on the floor. But it's impossible to ignite a fine, moist mildew. Blessedly, they went out.

Then Arthur would increase the sacrifice of my visit by first motioning toward a moist sofa of uncertain color, and then speaking deadly words: "Have a seat, why don't you, Reverend?"

From the beginning, I did not like to visit Arthur Forte.

Nor did he make my job (my ministry! you cry. My service! My discipleship! No—just my job) any easier. He did not wish a quick psalm, a professional prayer, devotions. Rather, he wanted sharply to dispute a young clergyman's faith. Seventy years a churchgoer, the old man narrowed his eye at me and argued the goodness of God. With incontrovertible proofs, he delivered shattering damnations of hospitals (at which he had worked), and doctors (for whom he had worked over the years): "Twenty dollars a strolling visit when they come to a patient's room," he said, "for what? Two minutes' time, that's what, and no particular news to the patient. They leave that sucker feeling low and worthless. God had listened to their heart, and didn't even tell them what he heard! Ho, ho!" said Arthur, "I'll never go to a hospital. Ho, ho!" And somehow the failure of doctors he wove into his intense argument against the goodness of the Deity. When I left him, I was empty in my soul and close to tears, and testy, my own faith in God seeming most stale, flat, unprofitable at the moment. I didn't like to visit Arthur.

Then came the days when he asked for prayer, Scripture, and Holy Communion, all three.

The man, by late summer, was failing. He did not remove himself from the chair to let me in (I entered an unlocked door), nor even to pass urine (which entered a chair impossibly foul). The August heat was unbearable. I had argued that Arthur go to the hospital. He had had a better idea. He took off all his clothes.

Naked, Arthur greeted me. Naked, finally, the old man asked my prayers. Naked, he opened his mouth to receive Communion. Naked. He'd raised the level of my sacrifice to anguish. I was mortified. And still he was not finished.

For in those latter days, the naked Arthur Forte asked me, his pastor, to come forward and put his slippers on him, his undershorts, and his pants. And I did. His feet had begun to swell, so it caused both him and me unutterable pain in those private moments when I took his hard heel in my hands and worked a splitbacked slipper round it; when he stood groaning aloud, taking the clothing one leg at a time; when I bent groaning so deeply in my soul. I dressed him. He leaned on me and I touched his nakedness to dress him, and we hurt, and his was sacrifice beyond my telling it. But in those moments I came to know a certain wordless affection for Arthur Forte.

(*Now* read me your words, "ministry," and "service," and "discipleship," for *then* I began to understand them: *then,* at the touching of Arthur's feet, when that and nothing else was what Arthur yearned for, one human being to touch him, physically to touch his old flesh, and not to judge. In the most dramatic terms available, the old man had said, "Love me.")

The last week of August, on my weekly visit, I found Arthur prone on the floor. He'd fallen out of his chair during the night, but his legs were too swollen and his arms too weak for climbing in again.

I said, "This, is it, Arthur. You're going to the hospital."

He was tired. He didn't argue any more, but let me call two other members of the congregation. While they came, I dressed him—and he groaned profoundly. He groaned when we carried him to the car. He groaned even during the transfer from cart to wheelchair: we'd brought him to emergency.

But there his groaning took on new meaning.

"I'm thirsty," he said.

"He's thirsty," I said to a nurse. "Would you get a drink of water?"

"No," she said.

"What?"

"No. He can ingest nothing until his doctor is contacted. No."

"But, water—?"

"Nothing.

"Would you contact his doctor, then?"

"That will be done by the unit nurse when he's in his room."

Arthur, slumped in his chair and hurting, said, "I'm thirsty."

I said, "Well, then, can I wheel him to his room?"

"I'm sorry, no," she said.

"Please," I said. "I'm his pastor. I'll take responsibility for him."

"In this place he is our responsibility, not yours," she said. "Be patient. An aide will get him up in good time."

O Arthur, forgive me not getting you water at home. Forgive us 20 minutes' wait without a drink. Forgive us our rules, our rules, our irresponsibility.

Even in his room they took the time to wash him long before they brought him drink.

"Why?" I pleaded.

"We're about to change shifts. The next nurse will call his doctor. All in good time."

So Arthur, whose smell had triggered much discussion in the halls, finally did not stink. But Arthur still was thirsty. He said two things before I left.

He mumbled, "Bloody but unbowed." Poetry!

"Good, Arthur!" I praised him with all my might. Even malicious wit was better than lethargy; perhaps I could get him to shiv a nurse or two.

But he rolled an eye toward me for the first time since entering this place. "Bloody," he said, "and bowed."

He slept an hour. Then, suddenly, he started awake and stared about himself. "Where am I? Where am I?" he called. I answered, and he groaned painfully, "Why am I?" I have wept at the death of only one parishioner.

Since the hospital knew no relative for Arthur Forte, at 11 P.M. that same night they called me. Then I laid the telephone aside, and I cried as though it were my father dead. My father.

Indeed, it was my father. Anguish, failure, the want of a simple glass of water: I sat in the kitchen and cried.

But that failure has since nurtured a certain calm success.

I do not suppose that Arthur consciously gave me the last year of his life, nor that he chose to teach me. Yet, by his mere being; by forcing me to *take* that life, real, unsweetened, bare-naked, hurting, and critical; by demanding that I serve him altogether unrewarded; by wringing from me first mere gestures of loving, and then the love itself—but a sacrificial love, a Christ-like love, being love for one so indisputably unlovable— he did prepare me for my ministry.

My tears were my diploma, his death my benediction, and failure my ordination. For the Lord did not say, "Blessed are you if you know" or "teach" or "preach these things." He said, rather, "Blessed are you if you *do* them."

When, on the night before his crucifixion, Jesus had washed the disciples' feet, he sat and said, "If I then, your Lord and Teacher, have washed your feet, you also ought to wash one another's feet. For I have given you an example, that you also should do as I have done to you. Truly, truly, I say to you, a servant is not greater than his master; nor is he who is sent greater than he who sent him. If you know these things," said Jesus, "blessed are you if you do them" (John 13:14-17). Again and again the Lord expanded on this theme: "Drink to the stinking is drink to me!" One might have learned by reading it . . .

But it is a theme made real in experience alone, by doing it.

And the first flush of that experience is, generally, a sense of failure, for this sort of ministry severely diminishes the minister, makes him insignificant, makes him the merest *servant,* the least in the transaction! To feel so small is to feel somehow failing, weak, unable.

But there, right there, begins true servanthood, the disciple who has, despite himself, denied himself.

And then, for perhaps the first time, one is loving not out of his own bowels, merit, ability, superiority, but out of Christ: for he has discovered himself to be nothing and Christ everything.

In the terrible, terrible *doing* of ministry the minister is born. And curiously, the best teachers of that nascent minister are sometimes the neediest people, foul to touch, unworthy, ungiving, unlovely, yet haughty in demanding (and then miraculously receiving) love.

Arthur, my father, my father! So seeming empty your death, it was not empty at all. There is no monument above your pauper's grave—but here: it is here in me and in my ministry. However could I make little of this godly wonder, that I love you?

House With a View
by C. Ellen Watts

The young realtor shook his head decisively. "You can't afford this area," he said, guiding his sleek little car through twisting private streets.

How do you know? I felt like retorting. We had asked for a house with a view. With mountains providing an everchanging backdrop and the city stretched for miles below, I just knew I would be inspired to write and write. Besides, we yearned for the quiet such a location was sure to provide.

We had contacted the realtor weeks earlier. In order for him to have some idea of what to look for, we had told him everything but our grandmothers' names. So I accepted his say-so and contented myself with craning for one last wistful look at the mountain.

We had given him ample time and "For Sale" signs appeared on nearly every block, but the realtor had surprisingly little to offer. We knew, too, that it was presently a buyer's market. Perhaps the realtor's apathy developed during our first visit when my husband offended him by saying we preferred to live in a mixed neighborhood. In our city "mixed" refers neither to color nor ethnic background, but to areas populated by people with varied life-styles and religious beliefs.

Our request was made inoffensively. But even his professional double-talk could not hide the distinct cooling of his attitude as he realized we were not in sympathy with the predominant local cult.

"That narrows it down some, of course," was his cryptic reply.

"Some" turned out to be considerable!

At the end of the day we had seen less than a dozen properties, and had been informed that most would be difficult if not impossible for us to buy.

It was crazy! We were not starry-eyed first-time buyers. Years of owning our own home plus spiraling market values had left us with adequate equity. The salary increase which came with my husband's promotion insured our ability to make higher monthly payments if necessary.

Discouraged, we returned to our motel and plunked the bulky realtor's "bible" down on the table before us.

"Keep this overnight and look for yourselves," he had suggested.

So for hours we pored over inadequate photographs and print we were barely able to read. Bedtime found us with a growing list of "possibles," twin headaches from having squinted so long, and increasingly negative thoughts. *God, we didn't want to move here anyhow. Are You sure You won't change your mind? Could we have been mistaken? Maybe You—*

But we knew Who had arranged the transfer. So we repeated our frustrations (At 11 p.m. He must have been anxious to hear them again!), asked once more for guidance, and wearily slept.

Our appointment the next day was for one o'clock, so we made plans to use the extra time to do some looking on our own. Since it was hardly appropriate to begin knocking on doors at 8 a.m., I looked for fresh ads in the morning paper while my husband went to the office.

"This one really sounds good," I said when he returned at 10.

"They all do," was his comment.

Nevertheless, since the house was for sale by owner, he phoned for an appointment but got a recording. I added it to our list and we spent the rest of the morning driving, looking, sometimes stopping. Ours is a sprawling city. Two hours later, without having seen much, we paused for a quick lunch before keeping our appointment with the realtor.

"There's just one left on the 'drive by' list. Shall we take time to see it?" my husband asked. I noticed it was the one listed by owner.

"We'll be late for our appointment."

He shrugged. "If he has no more to offer than yesterday, it can't matter."

We quickly found its location on the rumpled map which lay on the seat between us in the car. The property was in the area the realtor had said we couldn't afford. However, the price was well below our limit.

"It probably won't be much," I remarked as we rounded a corner into a beautiful hilly section. Then, spying the address: "Hey, this looks all right!"

As we stopped, a car further down the street backed up and a tall young man stuck his head out the window. It was the owner.

"Would you like to look at the house?" he asked.

Inside, before we had hardly begun to look around, we glanced at each other. I think we both knew then that it was our house and that God had directed us to it. That feeling was confirmed for me when I came to the room which was right for my study, looked out the window, and saw the beautiful mountain I had noticed the day before. Covered with a riot of fall colors, it seemed close enough to touch. A friend later remarked, "If this view doesn't fill you with inspiration, it's surely not God's fault!"

We kept our appointment with the realtor. On the way my husband asked, "What do you think?"

I countered with, "What do *you* think?"

"I think if that fellow hasn't come up with something pretty good, we'd better consider it."

"Me too."

The realtor had nothing further to offer—not a single house!

Experiencing a lightheartedness we had not had during the entire house-hunting trip, we drove back to where a thoughtful owner had left a key for us in the mailbox. For two hours we combed the place for possible flaws and found plenty—all of which could be remedied with elbow grease and paint.

When the owner returned and we found that the interest rate, payments, and everything else were in harmony with our budget, we knew for certain God had directed us. We bought the house.

I had wanted a home in a quiet neighborhood—this time with a view. God had abundantly supplied. My heart continues to fill with gratitude as I sit at my desk first thing each morning and "lift up mine eyes unto the hills, from whence cometh my help." My friend is correct; it should be a blessed and easy place in which to work.

For several months now I have been content. The mountain is still there, steady as a rock, now partially covered with late snow, the spring colors brilliant in places. I doubt if I will ever grow weary of gazing in that direction.

The quiet, too, is precisely what I needed. Most of the homes around us have spacious, well-kept lawns; many are far more elegant than ours. No one drives a noisy clunker in this neighborhood or yells at their kids. In fact, if you want to change the exterior of your house or add a tool shed, you have to ask a committee's approval. We're decorating our own house because we happen to like to (don't tell, but it's also because we can in no way afford a decorator), but I suspect we're in the minority.

On Sunday and prayer meeting night, we're a real minority. As Christians, isolated. I didn't think too much about it (I have my writing, you know) until God started talking to me about another view.

Between our house and the mountain lives a sad-faced widow who grooms her lawn while we worship. Beside her are people in their 50's who have no thought for church. Residing in the yellow split-level is a couple, each of a different nationality, neither speaking the other's language. Can a marriage survive under today's pressures with such severe limitations? With God's guidance it can, for sure. Across the street is an engineer with knowledge enough to have designed missile covers. I'm sure neither he nor his wife have a personal knowledge of Jesus. All around us are families bound to a cult which demands all from them, yet offers no peace of heart.

If I walk to the other end of the house and look out the dining room window I can see almost the entire metropolitan area. Beautiful—especially at night.

Half a million people live within my line of vision. Mind-boggling. The majority recently erected a new temple. On the outside are the words, "Holiness unto the Lord." Inside they follow the twisted teachings of a false prophet and practice weird rituals. Heart wrenching.

Yes, God is (note the present tense) giving me a view.

The mountain, I think, was a bonus.

John Calvin:
The Burning heart
by Sherwood E. Wirt

God, the late evangelist Joe Blinco often remarked, has a disturbing habit of laying his hands on the wrong man.

It could be said that God laid His hands on the wrong man in John Calvin. A think timid, dyspeptic Frenchman with a scraggly beard, Calvin was basically a scholar who desired nothing better than to spend his life in libraries. Instead, he was thrust into the vortex of Europe's fiercest religious battles. Before he died in 1564 at the age of fifty-four, he had met the challenge, overcome his opposition, and become one of the most influential figures in religious history.

But at a cost. For while his brilliant teaching, writing, and devout spirit had won the respect of millions, his angry polemics, vindictive diatribes, and mistakes of judgment made him one of the most maligned and vilified figures of his century.

Since apostolic times, no one in the history of the Christian church has had as many enemies as Calvin. They insulted him, set dogs on him, fired guns outside his house, and threatened his life. In the halls of government, he was not only attacked for his theology, but on trumped-up charges of immorality.

From *Christianity Today,* Nov. 1977. © Copyright 1977 by Christianity Today, Inc., 465 Gundersen Dr., Carol Stream, IL 60187. Used by permission.

However, Calvin responded in kind; his pen made him an opponent to be feared.

Yet there was a gentleness in Calvin not often mentioned. He knew how to retain the admiration and affection of his friends. During the twenty-seven years he was a pastor in Strasbourg and Geneva, he showed a sensitivity and love for his parish members that is a model for today's ministers. He was tender and affectionate with his wife, Idelette. In her pregnancy, he was solicitous, and heartbroken when their son died. Calvin was a man acquainted with grief.

What a strange man he was, but what an impact he made on his generation. Calvin was truly the architect of the Reformation. What Luther and Zwingli created, he set in order. He provided the disorganized Protestant community with a scriptural alternative to the medieval church. He revised the worship service, introduced congregational singing, regulated church discipline, and established a representative church government. He founded the University of Geneva. He laid the forms of political liberty in the western democracies by his insistence that God and God's Word stood above the state. Max Weber, the German social scientist, even accused Calvin of creating a "Protestant work ethic" that gave rise to capitalism.

But it wasn't what Calvin taught as much as the kind of people he produced that affected the future of the Christian world. Emile Leonard says that Calvin "invented a new kind of man in Geneva—Reformation man—and in him sketched out what was to become modern civilization." More than anyone, Calvin was responsible for the emergence of the "Puritan conscience" which first budded in Switzerland, then spread throughout Europe, including Britain and her colonies. "Calvinism" thus became a world force.

What was the essence of Calvinism? The chief characteristic of this "new man?" One might reply by quoting the five doctrinal points in the famed acronym TULIP—total depravity, unconditional election, limited atonement, irresistible grace, and perseverance of the saints. An admirer and disciple of Calvin in the last century, Benjamin B. Warfield of Princeton said, "The Calvinist is the man who has seen God, and . . . is filled on the one hand with a sense of his own unworthiness . . . and on the other hand with adoring wonder that nevertheless this God is a God Who receives sinners."

John Richard Green describes the effect of such teaching on sixteenth-century Europe: "The meanest peasant, once called of God, felt within him a strength stronger than the might of kings. In that mighty elevation of the masses embodied in the Calvinistic doctrines of election and grace, lay the germs of the modern principles of human equality."

Election and grace, chosenness and favor. Such theological convictions were woven into the sober, hard-driving character of the English Puritan, Scottish Presbyterian, French Huguenot, and Dutch Reformed immigrants of the new world. They caused the German historian Leopold von Ranke to remark, "John Calvin was the virtual founder of America."

Calvin, the man whom Rome feared more than Luther, was born in Noyon, Picardy, France, a loyal son of the papacy. As a boy he trained for the priesthood; later he studied law at Orleans. Either during the latter period or shortly after he had a "sudden and unexpected conversion experience." Not much is known about it; Calvin said simply that God "tamed him to teachableness."

Before long, Calvin's views were becoming known in French Catholic circles. In 1533 his Paris rooms were searched and his papers seized by the Inquisition. Using an alias, Calvin went underground, turning up in various cities in France, Germany, and Switzerland.

During his stay in Basel, the first edition of his *Institutes of*

the Christian Religion made its appearance, and the world saw
the doctrine of predestination which is the teaching Calvin is
best remembered for.

He was quite aware of its controversial nature. While taking
his family out of France under a safe-conduct in 1536, Calvin
took a circuitous route through Geneva to Strasbourg, Germany. When the Swiss reformer Guillaume Farel heard Calvin
was staying the night in Geneva he prevailed upon the young
refugee to stay and help establish the Reformation in Geneva.

The arrival of Calvin in Geneva was a fortuitous accident or
an act of God, depending on the measure of one's Calvinistic
inclinations. It might be said that not only was Calvin the
wrong man, but Geneva was the wrong city. But because Calvin's mark is still upon them, many disagree. They may differ
with much that he taught and did, but they can't escape him.

From 1536 until his death in 1564, Calvin exercised an increasing influence and control over the city of Geneva. For
three years, he was banished from the city, living and teaching
in Strasbourg. However, the city fathers found they couldn't
control Geneva without Calvin's wise counsel. Embassies
begged him to return, which he did reluctantly.

Under Calvin's guidance, the citizens turned Geneva into a
model community. Some of their laws seem laughable today,
but in Calvin's day no police force was needed there. Meanwhile the word spread abroad, and thousands of refugees
flocked to Geneva from the persecuted lands of Europe. They
sat at Calvin's feet as he taught the Bible. Yet Calvin held no
official position other than that of pastor and teacher. He avoid-
ed power and prestige, refused gifts, and lived in simplicity,
sleeping little and eating only one meal a day because of his
poor health.

Calvin lived in a cruel time. To recount his quarrels with his
theological opponents—Sebastien Castellio, Miguel Servetus,

and dozens of others—and the intolerance shown not only by Calvin but by church and civic leaders all over western Europe, would be like trying to clean a cesspool.

Servetus was executed for questioning the Trinity. Calvin could have spared his life had he wished, but chose not to interfere. Servetus, on the other hand, asked Calvin's pardon. The burning of Servetus haunts the memory of Calvin, though most Christian leaders of that day approved the verdict.

Calvin spent 458 pages of his *Institutes* discussing the knowledge of God. Yet he made scarcely a reference to love which, according to the Apostle John, is the one indispensible prerequisite to knowing God. Calvin knew what Jesus taught about love, but he never learned to love his enemies. So much for Calvinism in its extremest form.

But Calvin was not an extremist. He is still honored around the world. Much of what he taught about the Bible, culture, and human affairs has withstood the test of time. He built better than he knew.

Paul Wernle, the Swiss historian, says of Calvin, "We are all glad, no doubt, that we did not live under his rod; but who knows what we would all be, had not this divine ardor possessed him?"

Just before his death, Calvin told the ministers of Geneva, "I have always studied simplicity. I have written nothing through hatred against anyone, but have always set before me faithfully what I have thought to be for the glory of God."

On the day after his death, the magistrates, pastors, professors, and citizens of Geneva paid Calvin homage. At his request, he was buried in an unmarked grave.